ISBN 978-0-282-10297-5
PIBN 10239669

1 MONTH OF
FREE
READING

at

www.ForgottenBooks.com

By purchasing this book you are eligible for one month membership to ForgottenBooks.com, giving you unlimited access to our entire collection of over 1,000,000 titles via our web site and mobile apps.

To claim your free month visit:

www.forgottenbooks.com/free239669

English
Français
Deutsche
Italiano
Español
Português

www.forgottenbooks.com

Mythology Photography **Fiction**
Fishing Christianity **Art** Cooking
Essays Buddhism Freemasonry
Medicine **Biology** Music **Ancient**
Egypt Evolution Carpentry Physics
Dance Geology **Mathematics** Fitness
Shakespeare **Folklore** Yoga Marketing
Confidence Immortality Biographies
Poetry **Psychology** Witchcraft
Electronics Chemistry History **Law**
Accounting **Philosophy** Anthropology
Alchemy Drama Quantum Mechanics
Atheism Sexual Health **Ancient History**
Entrepreneurship Languages Sport
Paleontology Needlework Islam
Metaphysics Investment Archaeology
Parenting Statistics Criminology
Motivational

THE UNHAPPY VALLEY.

14067

BY

RICHARD F. BURTON,

LIEUT., BOMBAY ARMY.

Author of " Goa and the Blue Mountains," &c

IN TWO VOLUMES.

VOL. I.

LONDON:

RICHARD BENTLEY, NEW BURLINGTON STREET,

Publisher in Ordinary to her Majesty.

1851.

LONDON:
BRADBURY AND EVANS, PRINTERS, WHITEFRIARS

DEDICATION.

———•———

LIEUTENANT-COLONEL WALTER SCOTT,

BOMBAY ENGINEERS.

MY DEAR SCOTT,

THE sentiment may savour of Themistocles rather than Aristides; still I venture to hold that the pen in the hand of a man is that implement wherewith he may lawfully make known his obligations to those he loves, and, at the same time, answer loudly as he pleases certain other claimants to his attention.

Acting upon this principle—or no principle, as you please —I have inscribed these pages to you, a veteran dweller in the tents of Shem, a shrewd observer of all things oriental, and, what concerns my purpose infinitely more, an old and valued friend, whose claims to my gratitude I shall ever feel to be of the strongest.

LONDON, 1st August, 1851.

CONTENTS.

SCENES IN SCINDE.

CHAPTER I.

THE "𝔖𝔥𝔦𝔭𝔭𝔢 𝔬𝔣 𝔥𝔢𝔩𝔩𝔢"—*i. e.* THE GOVERNMENT
STEAMER THAT TOOK US TO SCINDE.

STEP in, Mr. Bull,—after you, sir!

I hope you liked Trafalgar, and Tarifa, and
Gibraltar, and Algiers, and Malta, and Alexandria,
and that you found the realities of travel almost as
entertaining as the thousand-and-one Di—, Pan—,
Physi—, Poly—, and other —oramic imitations at
which you have been perseveringly staring these last
few years, sir.

*   *   *   ⁀

You have now quitted Suez, which a facetious
"entertainer" very graphically described as being
the Grand Depot for the Overland Babies—you are
pacing the deck somewhat curiously and excitedly

as the steamer tears furiously down the middle of the Red Sea.

But you look in vain towards me, your guide. I will not answer a single question. One of these days, Mr. Bull, when you are quite recovered from the fatigue and annoyances of this Oriental trip, when Mrs. Bull once more allows you a few weeks leave of absence, when the boys and girls are all in rude health, and at work, as good children should be, and when there is no squabble, clerical, laical, on public grounds or on private grounds, in your happy home,—no murders in the neighbourhood to engross your attention and your spare time—then, sir, may be I shall offer my services as courier to you down the eastern coast of the Erythræan Sea up to Senaa in Yemen, the capital of that land of happy name.*

*   *   *   *

The " Semiramis," or some other confounded place of punishment with a high-flown misnomer, is in orders to convey from Bombay Harbour to Kurrachee a freight of 600 negro souls and bodies. Go we must, sir,—and by her, too; go we must. At this time of the year, October, a coasting voyage in a sailing vessel northwards, is a beautiful illustration of the Moral Impossible.

---

* Yemen—the " happy land."

" Hollo, young man ! where am I to put my box? Show me to my berth, will ye? And I say, don't forget I want that carpet-bag down in the cabin, and, O, yes, by-the-by, the hat-box must come too, —what the deuce is the matter with you ? "

Oh, Mr. Bull! Mr. Bull! what a sore and grievous *premier pas* is this! that gentleman whom you mistook for a steward, is the third lieutenant, an officer in the Bombay Marines, *alias* the Indian Navy, and an individual of infinite importance in his own estimation, if not in that of others. A subaltern in a steam-frigate, sir, is a regular sea-satrap—under authority, it is true, but not a whit the less capable of passing authority on with a mode and manner which render it extra-authoritative. Besides you have unconsciously touched a most sensitive " raw." He and all his cloth are rabid at the degradation of having to transport "soldier-officers," of being obliged to defile their spotless decks with " dirty passengers " and "filthy sepoys." The least allusion to this great grievance is sure to arouse a tornado of wrath in the blue-coated bosom. Now hearken to the thunder that bursts over your devoted head——

" Go to the D——, you old fool. I say, Quarter-master, pitch that fellow's traps overboard—sharp, d'ye hear?"—

Ending with a tirade of personal observations, not of a complimentary description.

Were the said lieutenant a fellow-passenger with you to Margate or Herne Bay, I should counsel you to invest a five pound note in revenge—not that you would require much advice about the matter.

But my dear, fat, old, testy, but very unblood-thirsty *papa de famille*, here—in these Eastern seas —all you can do is to swallow, with as few grimaces as possible, the bitter bit which you took into your mouth.

It is only four days to Kurrachee.

    *   *   *   *

We eat and drink like ghools or schoolboys on board the "shippe," because we pay one pound per diem for our " keep." We have literally nothing to do with, for, or to ourselves, and to eat and drink is, all things considered, less laborious than to do nothing. At six o'clock A.M. there is coffee on deck ; at nine we go down to breakfast ; at noon we assemble to "make it twelve" by the peculiar process of imbibing brandy and water and crunching sea-biscuits. At 3 P.M. we dine with the sub-alterns in the gun-room, I believe they call the place : we small fry cannot pass the dread portals of the " state-cabin," where sits the commander surrounded by his field officer-passengers. Three hours afterwards we again apply the spur to the jaded appetite, and take tea—a meal consisting of a devilled biscuit and pale ale; and from that time forwards we adhibit to ourselves as much liquid aliment as we can dispose of. Between whiles we smoke, generally cheroots, sometimes a hookah to feed the comical indignation of our nautical friends.

You have learned by this time, I presume, what ship cookery is—how the *potage* is always poultice-like pea-soup; how the bottles in the cruet-stand always contain "passenger-pickles" (*i. e.* so hot that an ounce lasts a year); how the bluish red or boiled-to-tatters mutton tastes exactly as if it had been cooked by the stokers in the engine-room; how politeness forbids the appearance of "salt horse" or pork, the only good things on board; and finally, how the fat steams of the vegetables remind you of nothing but a dirty *torchon*.

Your mental machinery is in a state of confusion, I see. You know not "what to observe," and would rather prefer observing nothing just at present. Very well, we will talk over matters to-morrow. So good night.

   *   *   *   *

We rise early, exactly at half-past 3 A.M., one

of your old favourites, the heroes of your juvenile
years—a " Jack Tar "—growls aloud,

" Tum'le out there, goin' t' wash dex,"—

And if you do not obey the order instanter, he
swamps you and your couch with a tubful of cold
water. The best joke the honest light-hearted
fellows know is to make a land-lubber thoroughly
miserable, no matter by what means.

Rising in your day-shirt, which does duty as
chemise de nuit, and certain cotton drawers called
pajammas—very useful when sleeping in public—
you choose a seat, the bulwarks, or any other
elevation inaccessible to the swirling streams which
overflow the quarter-deck ; there you rub your red
eyes with alarming violence, yawn like a little
crocodile, stretching all your limbs at the same time,
and ask and answer your friends sundry queries
concerning the last Indian Night's Entertainment.
When the dizziness of drowsiness leaves your brain
you essay a kind of ablution—not with the priggish
precision of a Bengalee, who commences to use the
tooth-brush in his verandah regularly at 3 A. M.—
yours is a catholic, syncretistic style of lavation,
performed, campaigning-fashion, in a tinned pan,
called a gendee. You are now in a proper state
of mind to look around you admiringly, to

enjoy the manifold charms of nature—such as the cool dewy breath of delightful morn, the cloudless welkin's azure depth, and the tiny undulations of the sapphire wave, streaked by the orient sun's aureate rays, and—perhaps you smoke a cigar——

You dress for breakfast and finish that meal rapidly, not relishing milkless tea or tincture of coffee, which on a pinch might serve for ipecacuanha.

The horrors of the day then begin in real earnest. You cannot sit in the rattling, creaking, groaning, shivering, steaming gun-room, full of the bouquet of dinner and sour bread. On deck there is an awning, but it is about as efficacious to protect you from Phœbus's fury as a lady's park parasol against a gin-palace on fire. You cannot read even if you had books; you cannot talk even were you inclined to do so. There are six hundred sepoys on board, each squatting on half-a-foot of deck, cramped, you may suppose, as to their limbs, but by no means fettered about that unruly member, the tongue. How they chatter, squabble, blow the conch, sing hymns to the sea-god, and smear themselves with oil of cocoa-nut! You wonder how the fellows keep life and body together upon a quantity of parched grain barely sufficient for a barn-door cock,*

---

* High-caste Hindus would rather starve than cook on board ship.

how they can be so cheerful without the accustomed hookah, and above all things, how they can sit by day and sleep away the night in the posture of a crow in the act of incubation.

The party contains a lady too; and however sweet the presence of the fair sex may be in its normal place, on board ship—ahem! Five gentlemen are paying her devoted attentions; numbers one and two walk arm in arm with her, each speaking in his own whisper; a third follows holding her parasol, another precedes her with her novel, and the fifth hangs about with her lap-dog—most of them are Irishmen; all are as fierce as fiends—it is not safe even to look that way.

You cannot walk; the only tolerable part of the quarter-deck belongs, by right of office, to the " monarch of all he surveys "—one as absolute too, as any Robinson Crusoe or French cook in his own empire—our captain. So wearily enough the perspiring Hours drag one foot after another as they limp through their monotonous *chaine des dames*. Do you not wish that we could hypnotize for three days like fakirs, or indulge in a triduan bout of hybernation, as the Esquimaux are said to do?

At last it is 11 P. M. We prepare to "turn in," if that technical phrase may be applied to depositing our persons upon the contents of these bundles— pillows, padded coverlet, sheets, and sleeping mat, spread on some unoccupied space, wherever the quarter-deck will receive us under its awning.

Now observe certain Anglo-Indianisms.

See how that young gentleman—a "fast" infant, who has been smoking all day, crushing and throwing away every second cigar with an air, drinking at least two gallons of ale, and yet complaining that he is "stinted in his liquor,"—undresses himself. Stretched upon his litter, and presenting the appearance of a spread-eagle couchant, he superintended the operations of unbooting, unsocking, and unpantalooning, as performed by Baloo, a "boy" * of fifty. Mr. Ensign Snooks's temper has been ruffled ; how, I cannot say, but the fact is unimpugnable. He does nothing but kick the said Baloo's shins, and indulge in curious physiological allusions to his (Baloo's) maternal progenitor, his wives, sisters, and the other ladies of his family. Not that the "boy" cares much about that matter, he has taken the "griffin"-line, angles for embryo commanders-in-chief, fleeces them for the few first months after their arrival in the country, convoys them to their first

---

* In western India the head servant is a "boy" all his life. Philologists differ as to the origin of the word.

"out-station," and turns them off when they begin to study Hindostanee.

Turn we to another picture—I may scarcely term it a smiling one.

For instance, that old captain, with a stock-fish complexion, and a forehead which looks as if the skin had been pinched up into a hundred wrinkles. He is going to grumble himself to sleep, and to enliven the last hours of discontented day by witnessing the dire discomfort of some sleepy black, who is ordered to shampoo the old benevolent's arms and legs till, to translate his own phrase, his "eyes turn white" with fatigue.

Or the fashionable major in her most gracious Majesty's —— regiment, *en route* to join his corps. He has been "friends" with almost everybody; he has edified the oldsters, astonished the youngsters, and delighted all hands by the number of titles his conversation contains, and by his anecdotes anent clubs, balls, steeple-chases, hunts, the "women," and the continent. He did not patronise ale, but the way in which he eyed, tasted, and rolled his head after each glass of bilious sherry or sour Bourdeaux, proved him to be quite a *gourmet.* See now the result of connoisseurship. The posterior portion of his bran-new Lincoln and Bennett lies crushed between his head and the pillow, whilst his catalepsed lower limbs refuse to remove the polished *chef d'œuvres* of Hubert, from the chests and faces of the neighbouring line of sleepers. " Snowball," his attendant pariah, kneels beside him in despair, and the amiable old captain involves in one comprehensive d——, all the Queen's officers ever created, with everything and everybody ever belonging to them, " Snowball " included.

You seem astonished, Mr. Bull, at the amount of revelling and the general dare-devil tone of things on board the " shippe." A word in your ear—

Those gentlemen are all going up on field service. Reports   *   *   *   The Sikhs   *   *   * The Affghans   *   *   *   Cashmere shawls *   *   *   Precious stones   *   *   * Two millions of pounds sterling in gold   *   *   *

        *   *   *   ‹

We go to bed, too, under the awning as usual. Recollect if it rains, which it is pretty sure to do, clutch up your bed, and do not walk, but bolt as fast as you can into the gun-room. If you are agile in your movements, you may chance to secure part of the table, or a quiet place under it. But mind, above all things, avoid sleeping on any part of the narrow strip of thoroughfare which runs round

that venerable piece of furniture, unless you wish to
have one of your favourite Ben Braces, or Tom
Starboards walking slowly over your countenance
with the thickest of ammunition boots. In the mean
time, make all preparations for covering yourself
with something warm. Hereabouts, if it is Jehan-
num by day, it is generally Barahoot * by night.
And particularly avoid sleeping in the moonlight.
Yon omniscient English gentlemen may laugh at
what I am going to tell you, still it is not the less
true. Many an incautious negro has risen in the
morning from his soft slumbers in " Cynthia's cooly
ray," with one moiety of his face by no means a
reflection of the other, and probably it took his
countenance a year or two to recover from the effects
of the moonblow.

Do you feel inclined to admire the unusual
brilliancy of the heavenly bodies—to speculate upon
the quantity of light which Jupiter affords — to
recognise the Bears, and dimly recollect that the poets
have said something about them—to, to—in a word,
to sentimentalise upon the sublime and beautiful?

"Not a bit!"

Well, sir, I thought so. The planks *are* rather

---

* The former the hot, the latter the cold place of eternal punishment,
selon Mohammed.

hard; the dew *is* somewhat chilly; that young fellow *does* snore a little, and that old gentleman *will* outcurse Ernulphus.

* * * *

Our course lies N. N. W., and all the first day we were in blue water, too far from the Northern Ocean and the coast of Guzerat to distinguish their several beauties. The wind, which at this season of the year is certain to be dead ahead, increased sensibly; in fact a gale seemed to be in prospect. But no one, I believe, ever passed the Gulf of Cambay without being in, or in the neighbourhood of, a storm. The second morning brought us in sight of the rounded headland and the little sand-hills which mark the position of Diu Fort, the name—famous in Western, infamous in Eastern annals,—of a place where Portuguese gallantry never shone more brilliantly, and where Portuguese treachery never appeared in blacker colours. A few hours after that the spires and towers, the bastions and bulwarks of the now ruinous settlement had disappeared from view, we shot by a shelving plain, the ancient site

"Of Somnath Puttan in Kattywar,"

as one of our bards geographically, but yet unmusically, sings, and the modern celebrity for having produced certain gates which afforded the periodicals and the public a great deal of innocent amusement.

There you caught a glimpse of the Land of the (self-styled) Children of the Sun and Moon, a nation of noblemen, whose pedigree dates, as you may guess from the family name, a great deal before the Conquest, and who, withal, have little but luminous origin, and a terrible habit of romancing to recommend them. Like the Belochies, the Welsh, and other semi-barbarous races, they actually support minstrels, an order of men whose only occupation is to scatter the dust of many "crams" over the venerable remains of antiquity, and to put together as many curious and elaborate lies as they can.

The scenery then becomes interesting enough. We stood within three miles of land, and every half hour supplied us with a change of prospect. The perpetually shifting coast was covered with towns and villages, here glittering in the sunshine, there almost concealed by surrounding wood, and the back-ground was a range of lofty hills whose forested crests, unconcealed by even the semblance of a mist, cut in jagged lines the deep blue surface of an Eastern sky.

*   *   *   *

At a distance you might mistake that tower for the spire of an old cathedral in good old Normandy

—it is the pagoda of Dwarka, a revered spot where some half million of pilgrims annually flock to spend their money, worship Krishna, receive the brand of that demi-deity, die of an epidemic, and feed the hungry sharks that haunt the bay in wait for devotee flesh. At night you remark the vast sheet of fire which spreads like lightning over the distant hills. They are covered with enormous bamboos, and these when dry are ignited by the friction which the wind causes, and burn with fiery fury. It is a favourite theme of the Hindoo muses—this Burning Jungle—and now that you have witnessed it, even from afar, you can well conceive how much glowing description and tenebrious terminology may be expended upon it.

The fourth morning we lose sight of land; we are striking across the Gulf of Cutch. Something *has* been said, and still there *is* something to be said, about the Kanthi of Ptolemy, the probability *versus* the possibility of the Runn ever having been an inland sea, the voyage of Nearchus and the accuracy or the errors of Arrian. But I have talked, heard, and written about the Kanthi and the Runn, Nearchus and Arrian, till the very names have become provocatives of qualm.

*　　　*　　　*

Here we are at last.   The extremity of that long line of blue hills lying to the northward is Cape Monze, a spot which, terrible to say, also has its debatable and debated classical name.* These insulated masses of stone which emerge a few feet from the water are the Oyster-rocks; they are to this region what the Needles are to the last bit of old England that detained our lingering looks.   When landing we pass between them and the craggy promontory, with the lighthouse on its walled summit—Fort Manhora.   This is the southern gateway of our unhappy valley, and the architecture and material—bleached and barren piles of limestone—have been admirably adapted by the hand of Nature to the luxuriant fields of marshy mangrove and salt sand which lie within the gorge. The rock rises about 130 feet perpendicularly above the level of the sea; it is nearly a mile in length, and towards the shore shelves down till it sinks into a muddy swamp, overgrown with vegetation, and over-flowed by every high tide.   Now, Sir, you stand a couple of miles from Kurrachee, the young Alexandria of our young Egypt,† and a few yards from the spot

* Eiros, I believe.

† " Young Egypt" is a favourite *soubriquet* for the Unhappy Valley, originating from an official proclamation, which announced the new conquest to be equal to Egypt in fertility.   Certainly, many parts remind one much of Amrou's despatch to the Caliph Umar, in which he describes the land of the Nile as successively appearing a desert, a lake, and a flower garden.

where British arms first showed the vaunting Scindee and the blustering Beloch what British arms can do when necessary.

As Sir J. K——, "after a service of forty-five years in the four quarters of the globe," was marching up to take the city, which made the knight a baron, he and his gallant soldiers were so evil entreated—at least, so it is said—by the Princes of the Indus, who would neither be on regular warlike terms with him, so as to give him an opportunity of looting * them, nor yet be sufficiently accommodating to assist him in looting others, that a reserve force was incontinently despatched from Bombay to be stationed in this favoured land, and to teach its rude rulers better manners.

Kurrachee was fixed upon as the point of disembarkation. H. M. ship "Wellesley," 74, and the "Hannah" transport, having on board H. M. 40th regiment, together with a company of artillery, arrived there on the 2nd of February, 1839, anchored under the walls of the fort, and summoned the garrison to surrender.

"I am a Beloch, and I will die first," was the magnanimous reply of the noble barbarian, the commander of the said garrison. Moreover, the same

---

* Loot is plunder in the Anglo-Indian dialect.

noble barbarian sent a few Scindee spies to "humbug" the British admiral and the brigadier into the belief that Manhora was a Gibraltar, and the Belochies perfect devils to fight.

"And so are we," quoth those not-to-be-humbugged personages.

Accordingly dispositions were made for the attack. The regiment and artillery landed, whilst the 74 cleared decks and was brought near for action. When all was ready, the fortress was a second time summoned, with true British humanity—it was supposed not to contain a farthing in copper—whereto it replied laconically and *tant soit peu* Gallicanly, that "Forts might be stormed, but they never surrender."

Under these circumstances, the "Wellesley" rejoined tartly, with a broadside, a hailstorm of bullets, which, as might have been expected, removed half of the miserable breastwork from its proud position above the watery plain into the watery plain.

After a few minutes' continued cannonade, the breach was reported practicable, and a gallant band—

"The full of hope, miscalled forlorn"—

pressed forward to claim the honour and glory of being permitted to die the hero's death.

"British officers and men," etc., etc., etc.——

Inflamed by the short and pithy harangue, the harangued moved on to the attack. Pausing for a moment to take breath at the foot of the rock, they scanned the summit with fiery looks; then, clambering up the steep side and tumbling over the wall and each other, with charging bayonets and the sturdiest possible hearts, they dashed impetuous into the midst of Fort Manhora.

What could withstand such gallantry? The garrison, an old man, a young woman, and a boy, instantly surrendered. So did the town of Kurrachee; so also did all the neighbouring districts.

The Governor-General of India "had much gratification in praising the forbearance both before and after the exertion of force" evinced by their excellencies the naval and military commanders, and the brave bands they commanded. Moreover, the same high functionary opined that the "prompt and effectual measures taken for reducing Kurrachee appeared to have been conducted in a manner such as to ensure success."

* * * *

I am telling you, Mr. Bull, the local, popular, and facetious version of the affair. Of course, there is another and a serious one. A great authority *

* "Narrative of the Campaign of the Army of the Indus in Sind and Kaubool."

in such things assures us that the flying garrison being captured, was found to consist of twenty men.

Allahu Aalam — the Lord is all-knowing, as the Moslem divines say, when compelled by circumstances to relate an apochryphal tale — may the penalty of fiction fall with all due weight upon the head of the fictor!

CHAPTER II.

FIRST GLIMPSE OF THE UNHAPPY VALLEY, AND THE NATIVE TOWN OF KURRACHEE.

" WELL, I never ! "

Of course not, sir. No one, man, woman, or child, ever saw the face of Young Egypt for the first time, without some such exclamation.

" A regular desert !—a mere line of low coast, sandy as a Scotchman's whiskers—a glaring waste, with visible as well as palpable heat playing over its dirty yellow surface ! "

Yes, sir—yes ! When last I went home on furlough, after a voyage round the Cape of Good Hope, the " Eliza " deposited me at Plymouth. In the pilot boat was an " old and faithful servant," from Central Asia, accompanying his master to the land of the pork-eater.

" Allah, Allah ! " exclaimed Khudabakhsh, as he caught sight of the town, and the green hills, and the woody parks, and the pretty places round about the place with the breakwater; "what manner of men must you Feringhis be, that leave such a bihisht * and travel to such accursed holes as ours, without manacles and the persuasions of the chob ! " †

You recollect, I dare say, Mr. Bull, reading in your Goldsmith, a similar remark made by one of your *compatriotes* in the olden time?

" Caractacus and Khudabakhsh be ——— !   Where are we to land here?   Where's the wharf?"

O man of civilisation, habituated as you are to quays and piers, with planks and ladders, I quite enter into the feeling that prompts the query. A long billowy sea, tipped with white, is sweeping directly into the narrow rock-girt jaw of the so-called harbour; we roll to such an extent that if you like the diversion you may run from one side of the quarter-deck to the other, each time dipping your fingers in the pure element; and to confuse matters still more, we have six hundred sepoys to land.

There is a bar across the creek; so the "Semiramis" must lie at anchor outside till the pilot boats put off to fetch us.

Here they come, anything but agreeable to look at, but capable of going strangely well, half-through

---

* Paradise.   † The bastinado.

half-over, the foaming waves. They are along-side, the chattering of the owners tells us.

The sepoys disembark first. There goes one of them into the sea, musket, knapsack, brass pipkin and all. If he were an Englishman how he would drop "Brown Bess," and kick, and plunge, and roar, and cry, "Save me!" But he is a Hindu. So, firmly grasping his weapon as if he were about to find it essentially useful in the depths of the ocean, he sinks—permanently.

At the sight and sound of the fatal plunge you, good honest man, long accustomed, in concert with Mrs. Bull, Master Billy, and all the junior Bulls, to vent your feelings audibly, when a little girl tumbles in an "act of equestrianism" against the well-padded barrier at Astley's, cannot help for the life of you, shouting "man overboard!" rushing about the deck, and other signs of excited benevolence.

Curiously enough, the surrounding blacks—the lost man's comrades and friends—eye your outlandish proceeding. They peep a little at the water, converse a great deal, and when their officers ask them what has occurred, respond brightly—

"Ramjee Naick drowned!"

They would be rather disappointed, I really believe, were that Ramjee to reappear. Besides he was a low-caste man; even he himself would have hesitated to rank himself in the scale of creation with the C. O.'s milch-goat.

But the fat old Moslem ayah, the major's lady's black Abigail, does not seem at all anxious to share the poor pariah's fate. See how she sticks to the ladder, clings to the rope, and fearfully scans the insolent waves that now bedew her extensive display of leg, now sink into a yawning abyss, deep in the centre of which lies the little boat where she is required to deposit herself. You also, when you reflect that you have shins, and you remember how much harder than flesh wood is, do feel that the descent in this case is by no means a facile one.

The Ayah starts and stares, stretches forward and shrinks backward, restretches and reshrinks, shrieks a little, swears for the benefit of the boatmen, and shouts "are bap"* for her own. Presently some one, in pure pity of her case, pushes her headlong from behind into the canoe as it rises quivering upon the crest of a mountain billow. Fear not, sir, there is no danger of her being hurt,—she assumes a hedgehog's shape with infinite ease : *teres atque rotunda*, she tumbles upon a pile of boxes and bags, extends her arms, fixes herself firmly by means of

---

* "O my father!"—a common native exclamation.

her claws, pulls the veil over her modest head once more, and once more commences the usual series of assertions concerning the legitimacy of the boatmen, and the general conduct of their female relations.

Now, sir, it is your time. Shake hands with your fellow-passengers and "hope to have the pleasure of seeing them again soon," so shall they pronounce you to be a "devilish good fellow," in spite of your black coat. Finish your ale, and prepare to quit the "Shippe of Helle" with all expedition.

We have been delayed a little. One of the pilot boats, becoming tired of her occupation, made a deliberate attempt to escape. The marine on guard, however, sent a bullet through the sail, so very close to the sailors' heads, that the design was abruptly futilised. Seated partly in the cranky canoe, partly in the drifting spray, we fly along, as if teaming old Neptune's drag over the watery hills and dales, glide beneath Manhora Fort, and, crossing the bar, acknowledge with a heartfelt "Thank goodness!" the mercy of finding ourselves in smooth water at last.

*   *   *   *

The "Port" of Kurrachee, you see, has no pretensions whatever to be called a port. The roadstead is dangerously exposed, and the creek which runs up to the town is too shallow to admit anything but flat-bottomed steamers and small native craft. As, however, the whole of this coast is deficient in harbours, and this, though bad, is probably the best it affords, it is much frequented.   Some years ago it was considered a place of extreme importance, and a number of enthusiastic Anglo-Scindians detected in its position and capabilities a natural value which, improved by art, would certainly at some time or other raise Kurrachee high above Calcutta in the scale of Indian cities.   The expenditure of public money was more than liberal, a little army was collected here, and as the niggard country provides scarcely sufficient grain to support its scanty population, the import trade became brisk and regular, and even the export improved.   Kurrachee, thus shoved forward, took the first step *en avant* by outstripping and almost depopulating the maritime towns around.   It was then resolved that she should have all advantages to aid her rapid progress. Accordingly a stone pier was designed to run from the town half way down the creek.   The work was undertaken, and would have prospered too had it not unfortunately sunk nearly as fast as it could be built.   Estimates were called for to show what expense would attend blowing up the bar, and extensive field-works and fortifications, intended to be a depot for the material of war against Central Asia generally, were ordered to rise from the barren plain.

However! Kurrachee is Kurrachee, and Calcutta is Calcutta still.

*

As we pass on, you observe the piles of oyster-shells that line the shore: those, sir, are the produce of our celebrated fishery; they are considerably larger than your natives and their contents are not quite so delicately flavoured: but they also afford a very barbaric pearl of dingy hue, somewhat larger than a pin's head. This source of profit, such as it was, has now been dried up, not by the "ignorance and folly of the Ameers," but by the stolidity of certain local officials, successors to that well-abused dynasty—and by the rapacity of certain black subjects, who contracted for the fisheries and mercilessly fished up every shell they could find. There are the carcases of some large vessels stranded upon the mud-banks about the creek, and moored in its centre you see twenty or thirty Grabs from Muscat, Buglahs from the Persian Gulf, Cottias from Cutch, and Pattimars and Botillas from Bombay.

The tide is out and we may thank the bit of pier that we have not to sit away some tedious hours in this uncomfortable unaromatic conveyance, to bestride the damp backs of brawny Scindians, or to walk with legs *au naturel,* and nether garments upon our shoulders, through nearly a mile of mud and water, averaging two feet deep, with plenty of sharp shells at the bottom, and aquatic roots which admirably perform the office of mantraps.

Now, Mr. Bull, our pilot has cast anchor—a large round flat stone, about three feet in diameter, with two holes in it, one for the cable, the other for a long sharp stick, the fluke. We will land if you please. It is 6 p. m.; the fine time for a walk, the horses can follow us, and the luggage is sure to find its way up to the bungalow. So while it is *en route* we will stroll through the native town, and afterwards along the military road to the cantonment.

*   *   *   *

Kurrachee, you must know, has been identified by some palæogeographers, with the Krokali of the Greeks: on the grounds, I believe, that it stands in a province called Kakraleh.

There is only one objection to the theory, which is, that Kurrachee was built about one hundred and fifty years ago. The town is a mass of low mud hovels, and tall mud houses with flat mud roofs, windowless mud walls, and numerous mud ventilators, surrounded by a tumble-down parapet of mud, built upon a low platform of mud-covered rock.* This is the citadel: it fines off into straggling suburbs below, extending far northwards, and terminating at the head of the creek.

On approaching Kurrachee, three of the senses receive "fresh impressions,"—three organs are affected, far more powerfully, however, than pleasantly, viz., the ear, the nose, and the eye.

The perpetual tomtoming and squeaking of native music, mingled with the roaring, bawling voices of the inhabitants, the barkings and bayings of the stranger-hating curs, and the streams of the hungry gulls, who are fighting over scraps of defunct fishes, form a combination which strikes the tympanum as decidedly novel. The dark narrow alleys through which nothing bulkier than a jackass can pass with ease, boast no common sewer: drainage, if you can so call it, is managed by evaporation, every inhabitant throws away in front of his dwelling what he does not want within, whilst the birds and dogs are the

---

* The clay hereabouts used as plaster is thrown into a pit, worked up to the proper consistency with water, mixed with finely chopped straw, and trodden under foot till ready for use. The straw acts as hair in English mortar; without it the bricks would crumble to bits in no time.

only scavengers. This, the permanent fetor, is here
and there increased by the aroma of carrion in such
a state that even the kites pronounce it rather too
high to be pleasant, and varied when we approach
the different bazaars by a close, faint, dead smell of
drugs and spices, such as one might suppose to proceed from a newly made mummy. You are familiar
with Boulogne, Cologne, and Rome: this you at once
feel is a novelty. The people are quite a different
race from what you have hitherto seen. The characteristic of their appearance is the peculiar blending
of the pure Iranian form and tint with those of the
Indian branch of the same family. Their features are
regular; their hair, unlike the lank locks of the great
Peninsula, though coarse is magnificent in quantity
and colour; the beard is thick, glossy, and curling;
and the figure is manly and well developed. The
mass of the population is composed of Mohana or
fishermen. The males are scattered about, mending
and cleaning their rude nets: the ladies are washing
fish in foul puddles, or are carrying the unsavoury
burdens homewards on their bare heads. There is
every convenience for studying their figures; the
dress of the ruder sex, consisting of only the Scinde
hat and a pair of indigo coloured drawers extending
from the waist to the knee. The women are habited

in a kind of embroidered boddice, called a " gaj," and long, coloured cotton pantaloons tightened round the ancle. They seldom wear veils in the streets, modesty not being one of their predilections; nor are they at all particular about volunteering opinions concerning your individual appearance, which freedom in the · East, you know, is strange. The Moslems are distinguished by their long beards, slipperless feet, and superior nakedness: Hindoos, by fairness or rather yellowness of complexion, a strangely shaped turban, a cloth fastened round the waist, a dab of vermilion between the eyebrows, and a thread hung over the left shoulder, and knotted against the right side. The descendants of African slaves abound: we meet them everywhere with huge water-skins on their backs, or carrying burdens fit for buffaloes.

All the people are preparing for prayers. The Hindoos are accurately washing their mouths, tooth by tooth, on the steps opposite their shops, or are purifying their sable locks and ochre skins with the mixture of argillaceous earth * and mustard oil which hereabouts is used for soap. The Moslems have spread their carpets, and are standing reverentially in

---

* It is called Met, and is quarried near Hyderabad and other places. The Persian name is Gil-i-Sar-Shui—" the head-washing clay." When mixed up with rose leaves, instead of rancid oil, it makes anything but a bad wash-ball.

the direction of Mecca with faces even graver than usual, and their hands raised to heaven.

"They turn towards the sun, are they worshipping it?"

"Man, man, what a question! And yet I have been asked it a dozen times by ignoramuses who have lived years and years in the East. No, Sir; they are praying very much as you do, or should do—only their devotions conclude with invoking the intercession of Mohammed their prophet. You might take a lesson, if not too proud to be taught, from their regularity in performing their religious duties; high and low almost all pray twice a day, some as many as five times, in public too, so that there may be no shirking. The working classes seldom understand much of what they are repeating, Arabic not being more intelligible to them than Latin is to a Frenchman or an Irishman. But *their* priests *will* allow them to peruse their Scriptures translated into the vernacular."

Let us leave this most olid town and pursue the path that leads towards the river—I forget what its name is, you must not expect to find water in it; although at times after heavy rains in the hills, the broad deep bed can scarcely contain within its wooded and gardened banks the rapid and muddy

torrent that runs down it, in autumn and winter
it is always dry.   Here and there, you observe,
remains a pool in which the little blacks are disporting themselves like dabchicks in their quasi-native
element.   In other places pits have been sunk, and
round the margins stand crowds of dames, fair and
dark, young and old, of high and low degree, each
with her earthen waterpot on her head and most of
them with infants that cling to their parents' sides
like baby baboons.   There is an immensity of confabulation going on, and if the loud frequent laughs
denote any thing beside vacancy of mind, there is
much enjoyment during the water drawing.   In the
East, you know, the well is the place of *réunion*,
and of *conversazione*, the " scandal-point," and the
pump-room of each little *coterie*.   The ladies there
prepare their minds for the labours of the evening,
such as cooking their husbands' and children's din-
ners, mending their clothes, preparing their beds,
and other domestic avocations multifarious.

Striking from the river bank, towards the cantonment, we pass some attempts at gardens, and thin
plantations of cocoa-nut trees, surrounded by dwarf
and broken walls of puddle.   Remark this man, a
tall Banyan,* whose long legs depend from that

---

* The pure Hindoo considers it a disgrace to mount an ass.   In Scinde,

diminutive donkey's saddleless crupper,—is he not like
an ourang-outang bestriding a Newfoundland dog?
That lofty clump on the other side of the road conceals a dry tank, and shelters some houses inhabited
by holy characters. It is called the Ram Bagh, or
Garden of Rama (Chandra),* as here, on this very
spot, the mighty hero and demigod of that name
passed a night some few million years ago, when he
and his pretty wife Sita were, like ourselves, Mr. Bull,
taking a trip through the Unhappy Valley of the
Indus. Now we have nothing to do but to follow
this exceedingly dusty and disagreeable highway
about half a mile, when we shall reach our destination and dinner.

How lovely are these oriental nights!—how especially lovely, contrasted with the most unlovely
oriental day. The plain around us is nothing but
an expanse of sand, broken into rises and falls by
the furious winds, and scarcely affording thorns,
salsolæ, and fire-plants,† sufficient to feed a dozen
goats and camels. Yet, somehow or other, the hour

however, the intolerance of the Moslem rulers compelled them to adopt
the lowly *monture*, and now, from force of habit, they would be unwilling
to exchange it for another.

  * So called to distinguish him from Parasu Rama, another heroic
incarnation.

  † The common name for the different varieties of Euphorbia.

communicates a portion of its charms even to this prospect. The heavy dew floats up from the sun-parched earth in almost transparent mists, that at once mellow, graduate, and diversify a landscape which the painful transparency of the atmosphere during daytime lays out all in one plane like a Chinese picture. The upper heights of the dome above us are of the deepest, purest, and most pellucid blue, melting away around its walls into the lightest azure; the moon sheds streams of liquid silver upon the nether world; there is harmony in the night gale, and an absence of every harsher sound that could disturb the spell which the majestic repose of Nature casts upon our spirits.

*   *   *   *

Before we enter our bungalow, and "shut up" for the night, I must remark concerning what we have just seen, that Kurrachee, (the native town,) wants many an improvement, which perhaps old Time, the great Progressionist, has in store for it. To him we look for the clearing of the harbour, the drainage of the dirty backwater, and the proper management of the tidal incursions. He may please to remove the mountains of old rubbish which surround and are scattered through the native town; eventually he may clear away the crumbling hovels which received us, at the head of the Custom House Bunder, and occupy the space with an erection somewhat more dignified. Possibly he will be induced to see the pier properly finished, to macadamise the road that leads to camp, to superintend the growth of a shady avenue or two, and to disperse about the environs a few large trees which may break the force of the fierce sea wind, attract a little rain, and create such a thing as shade. We trust implicitly in Time. Withal we wish that those who have the power of seizing him by the forelock would show a little more of the will to do so. The old gentleman wears a fashionable wig, curly enough in front, but close behind as a pointer's back; and we, his playthings, are always making darts at the wrong side.

CHAPTER III.

CAMP KURRACHEE AND ITS ENVIRONS. MUGUR PEER AND THE CROCODILE RIDE.

YOUR first night in Scinde, Mr. Bull—how did you like it?   I had your couch placed in the verandah—screened, however, from the sea-breeze, which is said to be dangerous—because you never could have endured the 100° heat of an inner room, and I now come to awake you at four A. M., and take you to constitutionalise a little before the sun appears.   The great secret of health in this part of the East lies, I believe, in the daily habit of a long walk, not a lazy canter, in the cool of the morning.

We can now, if you please, perambulate the camp, and devote the evening and the morrow to a few excursions in the neighbourhood.

Kurrachee is the head-quarters of the local govern-

ment, and the great station for European regiments.*
The cantonment stands on a slope, which rises
towards the east into a little chain of rocky hills.
The foundation is a hard, dry crust of sand, gravel,
and silt, thinly spread over beds of stone and
pebbles. As in all camps, there is a huge dirty
bazaar, full of shopkeepers and servants, soldiers and
sepoys, ladies of no virtue to speak of, naked
children and yelping curs—a scene strictly in the
Eastern low life style. There are large, roomy
barracks, oblong, single-storied buildings, dressed
with mathematical precision to the front, and
flanked by equally precise roads, two dozen different
guards scattered in all directions, immense commissariat stores, a Protestant church, with very
little outward show, a Roman Catholic chapel,
built palpably for effect, two or three burial-
grounds, a species of barn intended for the accom-
modation of the Drama, many mess-houses, an
iceless receptacle for Wenham Lake ice, a library
without books, a school-room in which Indo-
British children receive the elements of education,
and sundry private buildings where public duties
are performed. The streets, or rather roads,

* There are generally about 5000 men of all arms, European and
Native, at Kurrachee.

are level, dusty thoroughfares, averaging fifty yards in breadth, and the houses are separated by tall milk bush hedges, enclosing "compounds," * so called, I presume, because the thing is a mixture of the garden and the court-yard.

Each domicile speaks plainly enough for its tenant. Here the huge white stuccoed pile, with tall arches and bright chiks † between, towering above a screen of Euphorbia, which takes the labour of a dozen men to water it, denotes the Commissariat or the Staff Officer. There the small, neat building, with carefully curtained windows, a carriage under the shed that adjoins it, comparatively clean out-houses, and an apology for a garden kept up in the face of many difficulties, points out the married captain, or field-officer. A little beyond it, another bungalow, jealously trellised round with bamboo-work, a gaudy palanquin lying near the dirty huts, and two or three jaunty, debauched looking "darkies," dressed in the height of black dandyism, show manifest traces of the " Booboo." ‡ Beyond it you remark a long, low range of stained and dilapidated building, under whose narrow verandah, with the

---

* Philologists derive the word from the Portuguese.
† A kind of fine mat.
‡ Beebee, a lady, is corrupted by the natives of western India, to Booboo, almost invariably when they speak of one of their own ladies.

rough wooden posts, still sleep three or four young
gentlemen, in spite of the glistering of morning, the
yelping of a dozen terriers, and the squabbling of as
many Pariah servants, each exhorting his neighbour
to do *his* work : that is a Castle of Indolence in which
several subalterns in one of her Majesty's corps chum
together, for the greater facility of spending days.
Again, you observe a mean-looking bungalow, with
appended kennels and stables, that are by far the
best part of the house : the fine head of an Arab
peeping out of his loose box is the only sign of life
about the place—that is a Duck " Subaltern Hall."
Both these establishments are apparently in a state
of admirable disorder : the fences are broken down
by being leapt over, the garden destroyed by being
galloped over, the walls pitted with the pellet-bow, *
and near each a goodly heap of dirty " Marines,"
who have travelled from the generous vineyards of
" the South " to do their duty on the parched plains
of Scinde, is piled close by shattered six-dozen
chests, old torn fly-tents, legless chairs, and other
pieces of furniture which have suffered in the wars
within.   The few pretentious erections, built in no
earthly style of architecture, which puzzle you as to
their intentions, are the " follies " of Anglo-Indian

* A bow which shoots clay pellets instead of arrows.

clerks and writers, a race of men which hugely delights in converting rupees to unlovely masses of brick and mortar. At first glance, your eye detects the humble dwellings of the primitive colonists, sheds of "wattle and dab," in the form of a single piled tent, for the most part now degraded into stables or servants' offices. They form remarkable contrasts with the double-storied houses, the thickly stuccoed roofs, made to be promenaded upon, and the extensive ranges of rooms, which have sprung up during the last ten years, when men could calculate upon being stationary for a while in the "station" of Kurrachee. Except in a few instances, all the tenements are bungalows, parallelograms of unlovely regularity, with walls of sun-dried brick, doubly white-washed to promote cleanliness and glare, sometimes flat above, more often sloping with red and blue tiles, with eaves pulled out, and prevented from falling by clumsy columns of brick. Each has its dependent line of dirty, dingy "cook-houses," dens for the servants, and other conveniencies thrown far enough off to temper the pungency of the screamings and the steams that escape through the doorless doorways.

Crossing the camp in a northward direction towards the Government Gardens, we pass through,

you observe, the heart of the settlement. Every thing
at this hour looks and sounds intensely military.
Yonder, on the regimental parade-ground, a plump
of glittering bayonets is wheeling and turning about
in close column; a little way in front of us a troop
of horse artillery winds slowly along the road
towards the Champ de Mars; in the square on our
right are some hundred " Johnny Raws " under the
Adjutant's watchful eye, in every grade of recruitism,
from the rigid miseries of the goose-step, to the last
touch of the sword exercise; and on the left a
native corps, with band playing and colours flying,
returns from drill to their lines and breakfasts.

This, Mr. Bull, is one of the Sepoy regiments,
about which you have heard so much of late. You
are right; there is something uncommonly grotesque
in their general appearance—a total want of " fitness
of things " in an Ultra-European dress, upon an
Ultra-Asiatic person. The men's shoulders are
rather narrow, their bodies are shortish, their waists
are waspish, and their thin legs appear to grow out
of their chests. Still they are stout hearts, and
true, these fellows; they have fought for your cotton
and pepper many a year, and you may still rely upon
their faith and loyalty. Ere long, I dare say, you
will hear of a torrent of them pouring westward

through Egypt, and I venture to assert that they will rather astonish the natives of Southern Europe. One company of them as they are is worth half a battalion of Italians or Greeks, and when they have a few more British officers to lead them on, you may safely trust them to act against any army whatever.

All around us there is a regular "Dutch concert" of martial music. Bugles are sounding light infantry calls—bands are performing whilst their regiments parade;—there is a rattling treble of musketry, a booming bass of cannon, and a practising of the drum, beat in the very soprano key which combines to form a perfect "Devil's Tattoo."

This position, in the outskirts of the camp, was chosen for the Government Gardens as it is the only place that affords a sufficient quantity of sweet water. The acre or two of ground thus grandiloquently designated, contains a multitude of wells, shady alleys for promenades, a chunamed* floor for dancing *au clair de la lune*, a square where the bands play to the ladies in the evening, a few flower-plots and a vast number of onion, lettuce and cabbage-beds. One walk through will suffice.

And now to breakfast.

*　　　　*　　　　*　　　　*

The sun is sinking slowly towards his purple

---

* Made of chunam or gypsum.

couch, the western main; we have still time to
canter over the couple of miles that separate us
from "Clifton."

Our route is exactly the opposite one to that we
followed this morning. Now you see the "West
End" of Kurrachee, where the Staff Lines are, where
great men dwell and where His Excellency the
Governor, or the Commissioner, as the case may be,
—titles are frail things here—holds his little court.
That strange looking building without windows, is
the Freemasons' Lodge, the *Jadoo Ghur*, or "Magic-
house," as the natives call it, considering the respectable order a band of sorcerers who meet in their
φιλαδελφειον to worship the Shaitan and to concert
diabolical plans and projects against Allah's chosen
people, themselves. This is the vulgar idea. The
more learned Orientals consider freemasonry a relic
of Guebrism imbedded in the modern structure of
Christianity. It is the fashion, I may observe, for
free-thinking Moslems to hold the Emperor
Aurelian's opinion that, "among all the Gods, none
is truly worthy of adoration but the sun." Impressed
with the truth of this theory, it is no wonder,
Mr. Bull, that their minds detect lurking Guebrism
in everybody's belief.

Clifton! How many recollections are conjured

up by the sound of the word. Again you see the
Tempe of old England with its turfy downs, its
wood-grown chasm, and its classic stream :

> "Tanto ricco d'onor quanto povero d'onde." *

Clifton ! you exclaim, in doggrel, for poetical you
may not become—

> "Powers of heaven ! and can it be,
> That this is all I am to see ?"

Yes, Mr. Bull, we are in Scinde, sir: a barren
rugged rock rising a few feet above the level of a
wretched desert plain close to the sea, and supporting some poor attempts at human habitations, say
a dozen villa-bungalows,—such are the uncomely
features of Clifton in the Valley of the Indus.

However the air is fresh and pure here, and the
denisons of Kurrachee consider I assure you a week
spent at this "watering-place" no small luxury.
Most of the regiments have houses or pitch tents
upon the hill. The bathing, too, is good. Piles have
been driven into the water so as to form a barrier
against the ravenous sharks that infest these seas
and to prevent the soldiers drowning themselves

---

* Said of the river Sebeto—

> "Overflowing with honor as scanty in stream."

by displays of natation. The great inconvenience of this Clifton is that as it affords absolutely nothing, not even fresh water; you must send to Kurrachee for all you want, and your servants have a pleasant knack on such occasions of invariably taking six to do what ought to occupy two hours.

There has been a large tiffin in that bungalow. Now watch proceedings.

A dozen young gentlemen smoking like chimneys at Christmas, talking and laughing at the same time, mount their Arabs, and show how Arabs *can* get down a puzzling hill. They all draw up in a line upon the bit of beach which separates the sea from the rock. There is a bet upon the *tapis* there.

A prick of the spur and a lash with the whip: on go the Arabs dashing like mad towards the water.

A long concave wave curls as the line nears the margin, and shivering bursts in a shower of foam; of the twelve horsemen only one has weathered the storm, kept his seat and won the day. The eleven others may be seen in various positions, some struggling in the swell, some flat upon the sand, and others scudding about the country, vainly endeavouring to catch or to curb their runaway nags.

*   *   *   *

It is time to return home. We had better skirt

along the shore and then strike into the fashionable drive, a long path marked out by hoofs and wheels over the barren undulations between the Staff Lines and the sea. There are carriages and horsemen, ladies and gentlemen, in abundance; uniforms meet you at every step. Brigadier Dunderhed is pleased to be particular at present upon the article of "harness." You see even the station "devil-dodger," as his reverence is irreverently termed by the sub-alterns, bestrides his old grey Rosinante in the costume of his order—a black tail coat, and a beaver covered over with white calico. We look rather "small" amidst this moving multitude of men in pink, and uncomfortably remarkable in our "mufti." So as I am not over anxious to receive a lengthy and artistic "wig," duly prepared and accurately fitted for, and viciously hurled at my pericranium by the outraged Brigadier, we will, if you please, retire into the obscurity of our private abode.

*　　　　*　　　　*　　　　т

Now, sir, up with you! on with the shooting jacket, the turbanded and wadded hunting-cap, the antigropiloses, and the cigar case that contains at least five bundles of Manillas. Our tent by this time must be pitched at Mugur Peer, and we have nine miles of bad ground to finish before we reach food.

The "Alligator Tank," as it is called by the natives, owes its origin and fame to one Hajee Mugur, a Moslem hermit, who first settled in the barren spot, and, to save himself the trouble of having to fetch water from afar, caused a rill to trickle from the rock above. It was visited by four brother saints who, without rhyme or reason, as Mrs. B. would say, began to perpetrate a variety of miracles. One formed a hot mineral spring, whose graveolent proceeds settled in the nearest hollow, converting it into a foul morass; another metamorphosed a flower into an animal of the crocodile species; and the third converted the bit of stick he was wont to use as a tooth-brush into a palm-shoot, which, at once becoming a date-tree, afforded the friends sweet fruit and pleasant shade. When his time was up, the "oldest inhabitant" paid a certain debt of nature to a certain inexorable old dun, and departed *en route* for Firdaus,* leaving his hallowed remains to be interred by the fraternity close to the scene of their preternatural feats.

After gallopping over a sandy and sterile tract, dotted with cactus and asclepias, we climb up the Pubb Hills, that line of limestone rocks which bounds the northern extremity of the Kurrachee desert, and abuts

* Paradise.

at Cape Monze, we thread our way through boulders of rock, and tread cautiously over sheets of flint, polished like glass by the feet of Scindee travellers, we descend a rugged path and descry in a ravine beneath us the oasis, containing a thick grove of palms, and the domed mausoleum of the holy Hajee. The morning sun upon an empty stomach has all the effects of a glass of lukewarm water after a good dinner, so we had better sit down at once to the duty of recruiting exhausted nature. Besides, I see we shall have to shift our tent. The careless wretches our domestics have pitched it under a thick and spreading tamarind tree. The natives of the country assure us that a night in its cool shade is certain to be followed by a fever in the morning. Once, and but once, to shame them out of their superstition, I tried the experiment in my proper person; but, Mr. Bull, like the prejudice-assaulting commercial gentleman who built a ship, called it "Friday," sailed it on the seaman's unlucky day, and lost it, the consequence of my little attempt was an ague, which made me quite as credulous upon that point as my informers were.

*　　　*　　　*　　　*

We are in luck. There is a *melo* or Pilgrim's Fair at the Saint's tomb, and a party of picnic-ers from Kurrachee: so we may calculate upon seeing some

sport. The *tout ensemble* of the scene strikes your
eye strangely, the glaring blue vault above vividly
contrasting with the withered and sickly foliage of
the palms which are now shedding their clusters of
bright gamboge-coloured dates; the quaintly habited
groups of visiters, the vivid emerald hue of the
swamp, intersected by lines of mineral water, and
covered with the uncouth forms of its inhabitants,
sluggish monsters, armed with a coat of mail composed of clay whitened and hardened to pottery by
the rays of the sun—all *hors de tenue*, like a black
woman dressed in red,* or a fair one in black and
yellow. The little bog before us, though not more
than a hundred yards down the centre, by half that
breadth, contains hundreds of alligators of every size
from two to twenty feet. But here comes the guar-
dian angel of the place, a tall, swarth, bony, fierce-
looking old fakir, who lives upon the offerings made
to the soul of Hajee Mugur. He wishes to know if
we will sacrifice a goat, and try the effect of a meat
offering to Mor Sahib—Mr. Peacock—the title which
the biggest of the monsters bears.

In the dark recess formed by a small bridge built
over the narrow brick canal which supplies the

* The Persians have a proverb, that a black woman dressed in red is
enough to make a jackass laugh.

swamp, and concealed from eyes profane by the warm, blueish, sulphureous stream, lurks the grisly monarch of the place. An unhappy kid is slaughtered with the usual religious formula, and its life-blood is allowed to flow as a libation into the depths below. A gurgling and a bubbling of the waters forewarn us that their tenant has acknowledged the compliment, and presently a huge snout and a slimy crimson case, fringed with portentous fangs, protrude from the yawning surface.

Wah! wah!!—hooray! hooray!! shouts the surrounding crowd, intensely excited, when Mr. Peacock, after being aroused into full activity, as his fierce, flashing, little eyes and uneasy movements denote, by a succession of vigorous pokes and pushes with a bamboo pole, condescends to snap at and swallow the hind quarter of a young goat temptingly held within an inch of his nose.

"Verily your prayers are acceptable, and great will be your fortunes in both worlds," solemnly remarks the old fakir, at the same time confiscating as his perquisite the remnant of the slaughtered animal.

I regret to observe, that we are not exactly in the most respectable society, dear Mr. Bull. Most of our fair fellow pilgrims are kanyaris, or dancing girls from Kurrachee, and even modest women here allow themselves a latitude of demeanour, usual enough at sacred places, but still, quite the reverse of the strictly proper. During the anxious moment which decides whether the alligator will or will not bite, eagerness gets the better of etiquette, faces are unveiled, and heads are bared in most unseemly guise. The groups that stand round the body of the swamp, throwing stones and clods of earth at its inhabitants, are too much frightened, when one of the minor monsters sallies forth in grumbling wrath, to think of anything but precipitate escape. And in the adjoining spring, a bevy of African dames and damsels are laving their uncomely limbs with the quantity of attire which would decently conceal a hand.

Should you like to see a Seedy-nautch.*

Very well, I will give the necessary orders.

The preparations are speedily made. A variety of fantastic flags are planted in the ground, and the musical instruments—a huge dhol or kettle-drum and sundry horns—are deposited in the shade of the tall tamarind. As dancing is a semi-religious rite, the performance commences with a burnt-offering of

* Seedy (a corruption of the Arabic سيدي, "my lord !") is the popular name in India for African blacks.

frankincense; the musicians then strike up, roaring a recitativo, tom-toming, trumpeting, and drubbing the drum, with the whole might of their loud, leathery lungs, and all the weight of their monstrous muscular arms.

Here comes the *corps de ballet*. It is composed of any number of dancers, male and female. At first the sexes mingle, each individual describing a circle of pirouettes, without any such artifice as time or step, round the central flag, and chaunting rude ditties with hoarse and willing throats. Then the figurantes separate themselves from the male artistes, and assemble themselves together—fascinating group!—whilst one of the number advances coquettishly, wriggling her sides with all the grace of a Punjaub bear, and uttering a shrill cry,* which resembles nothing but the death-shriek of a wild cat. After half an hour expended by a succession of ladies in these *pas seuls*, the fascinated host of male *vis-à-vis* can contain itself no longer within the bounds of quiet. They plunge forward, prancing, stop short, squat suddenly upon the ground, spring up and wave their arms, shouting and howling all the time more like maniacs than common mortals; the perspiration pours down their naked forms, they

* Called in Persian "kil,"—in Egypt, if I recollect right, "zugharit."

pant and puff most painfully; still they continue the performance. At times it is necessary to remove one of the gentlemen, who may have fainted from fatigue, over-excitement, and possibly, strong waters. His ankles are seized by the nearest pair, who drag him testily out of the ring, squeeze a wet rag over his prostrate form, and then leave him to "come round" when he can. The moment that he opens his eyes, be sure that, game as a bull dog, he will return to the charge, and dance himself into another fit with all possible expedition.

Ye admirers of the olden time, ye classical lauders of hoar antiquity, will you excuse me if I venture upon one query?

When those heavenly maids, Music and the Ballet, first came down from Olympus, condescending to take an engagement with young Greece, did they, think ye, appear in the primitive, natural, unaffected forms which they still display to ecstaticise the Seedy sons of youthful Egypt? I humbly opine they did. What say you, Mr. John Bull?

*   *   *   *

Now there will be something to laugh at. Out of the neighbouring tent sallies a small but select body of subalterns, in strange hats and stranger coats. They are surrounded by a pack of rakish-looking bull terriers, yelping and dancing their joy at escaping from the thraldom of the kuttewala.* There is a gun, too, in the party.

They seem just now at a loss what to do. They wander listlessly among the date trees, wink at the ladies, "chaff" the old fakir a little, offer up the usual goat, and playfully endeavour to ram the bamboo pole down Mr. Peacock's throat. The showman remonstrates, and they inform him, in a corrupt dialect of "the Moors," that he is an "old muff."

A barking and a hoarse roaring from below attract their attention; they hurry down towards the swamp and find their dogs occupied in disturbing the repose of its possessors.

"At him, Trim! go it, Pincher! five to one in gold mohurs that Snap doesn't funk the fellow: hist 'st 'st, Snap!"

Snap's owner is right, but the wretched little quadruped happens to come within the sweep of a juvenile alligator's tail, which with one lash sends him flying through the air into the "middle of next week."

Bang! Bang!

And two ounces of shot salute Snap's murderer's eyes and ears. Tickled by the salutation, the little

* The dog-boy.

monster, with a curious attempt at agility, plunges into his native bog, grunting as if he had a grievance.

Again the old fakir, issuing from his sanctum,—that white dome on the rock which towers high above the straggling grove,—finds fault with the nature of the proceedings. This time, however, he receives a rupee and a bottle of Cognac—the respectable senior would throttle his father, or sell his mother, for a little more. So he retires in high glee, warning his generous friends that the beasts are very ferocious and addicted to biting.

When "larking" does commence, somehow or other it is very difficult to cut its career short. No sooner does the keeper of the lines disappear, than the truth of his caution is canvassed and generally doubted. The chief of the sceptics, a beardless boy about seventeen, short, thin, and cock-nosed—in fact the very model of a guardsman—proposes to demonstrate by experiment "what confounded nonsense the chap was talking." A "draw it mild, old fellow," fixes his intentions.

The ensign turns round to take a run at the bog, looks to see that his shoes are tightly tied, and charges the place right gallantly, now planting his foot upon one of the little tufts of rank grass which protrude from the muddy water, now lighting on an alligator's back, now sticking for a moment in the black mire, now hopping dexterously off a sesquipedalian snout. He reaches the other side with a whole skin, although his pantaloons have suffered a little from a vicious bite: narrow escapes, as one may imagine, he has had, but pale ale and plentiful pluck are powerful preservers.

A crowd assembles about the spot; the exultation of success seems to turn the young gentleman's head. He proposes an alligator ride, is again laughed to scorn, and again runs off, with mind made up, to the tent. A moment afterwards he reappears, carrying a huge steel fork and a shark hook, strong and sharp, with the body of a fowl quivering on one end, and a stout cord attached to the other. He lashes his line carefully round one of the palm trees and commences plying the water for a mugur.*

A brute nearly twenty feet long, a real Saurian every inch of him, takes the bait and finds himself in a predicament; he must either disgorge a savoury morsel, or remain a prisoner; and for a moment or two he makes the ignoble choice. He pulls, however, like a thorough-bred bull-dog, shakes his head, as if

* An alligator.

D 3

he wished to shed it, and lashes his tail with the energy of a shark who is being beaten to death with capstan bars.

In a moment young Waterton is seated, like an elephant driver, upon the thick neck of the reptile, who, not being accustomed to carry such weight, at once sacrifices his fowl, and running off with his rider, makes for the morass. On the way, at times, he slackens his zigzag, wriggling course and attempts a bite, but the prongs of the steel fork, well rammed into the soft skin of his neck, muzzle him effectually enough. And just as the steed is plunging into his own element, the jockey springs actively up, leaps on one side, avoids a terrific lash from the serrated tail, and again escapes better than he deserves.

Poor devils of alligators—how they must ponder upon and confabulate about the good old times that were ! Once, jolly as monks or rectors, with nothing in the world to do but to eat, drink, sleep, waddle, and be respected ; now pelted at, fished for, bullied, and besieged by the Passamonts, Alabasters, and Morgantes of Kurrachee. Poor devils !

> *   *   *   *

As we return home we pass by one of the subterraneous aqueducts called Kareez used for irrigation throughout Central Asia. It is formed by sinking a

number of shafts at intervals of about twenty yards;
between each, a narrow tunnel is excavated ten or
twelve feet below the surface. Thus the inequalities
of level are overcome, and water is brought down
from the hills without evaporation, or, what is still
more important, without its being liable to be drawn
off by strangers before it reaches the owner's land.
The shafts are useful for repairs as well as excava-
tion: the long line of earthmounds, indicating the
several apertures, is a strange feature in a Scindian
landscape. This Kareez was dug by a native of
Kelat, who, in order to attract public attention,
offered to bring down a copious stream of water
from the Pubb hills. It is wonderful how accurately
the mountain people can judge by the eye the rise
and fall of ground, and how skilfully they manage
to excavate with most inefficient implements. This
attempt, however, ended in failure, probably because
the director of the works did not find it worth his
while to continue them.

CHAPTER IV.

THE MARCH AND THE VERY PRETTY PERSIAN GIRL.

WE must remain at Kurrachee for a week or two. Land travelling in these regions requires something more than the simple preparations of a portmanteau, a carpet-bag and a hat-box, and before the subsidence of the river* you might as well journey for pleasure through Central Africa as through the Valley of the Indus.

*   *   *

I thought you would not long escape one of the scourges of this wretched country—a dust storm.

When we arose in the morning the sky was lowering, the air dark; the wind blew in puffs, and—unusual enough at this time of the year—it felt raw and searching. If you took the trouble to look towards the hills about 8 A.M. you might have seen a towering column of sand from the rocky hills mixed with powdered silt from the arid plains, flying away fast as it could from angry puffing Boreas.

---

* In September and October.

The gale increases—blast pursuing blast, roaring and sweeping round the walls and over the roofs of the houses with the frantic violence of a typhoon. There is a horror in the sound, and then the prospect from the windows! It reminds one of Firdausi's vast idea that one layer has been trampled off earth and added to the coats of the firmament.* You close every aperture and inlet, in the hope of escaping the most distressing part of the phenomenon. Save yourself the trouble, all such measures are useless. The finer particles with which the atmosphere is laden would pass without difficulty through the eye of a needle; judge what comfortable thoroughfares they must find the chinks of these warped doors and the crannies of the puttyless munnions.

It seems as though the dust recognised in our persons kindred matter. Our heads are powdered over in five minutes; our eyes, unless we sit with closed lids, feel as if a dash of cayenne had been administered to them; we sneeze like schoolboys after a first pinch of "blackguard;" our epidermises are grittier than a loaf of provincial French bread, and washing would only be a mockery of resisting the irremediable evil.

---

* Moslems suppose that there are seven earths and seven heavens, disposed like the coats of an onion.

Now, Mr. Bull, if you wish to let your friends and old cronies at home see something of the produce of the East, call for lighted candles and sit down to compose an "overland letter." It will take you at least two hours and a half to finish the four pages, as the pen becomes clogged and the paper covered every few minutes; moreover, your spectacles require wiping at least as often as your quill does. By the time the missive comes to hand, it will contain a neat little cake of Indus mud and Scinde sand moulded in the form of the paper. Tell Mrs. Bull that you went without your tiffin—lunch, I mean—that you tried to sleep, but the novel sensation of being powdered all over made the attempt an abortive one,—that it is impossible to cook during a dust storm,—and that you are in for a modification of your favourite "intramural sepulture," if the gale continues much longer. However your days are safe enough; the wind will probably fall about five or six in the afternoon,—it is rare that it does not go down with the sun— and even should it continue during the night, it will be a farce compared to what we are enduring now.

.　　　　*　　　　*　　　　*

Kurrachee is celebrated for healthfulness; the

heat being at least twenty degrees* less on an
average throughout the summer hereabouts than in
Upper Scinde. Moreover, there is a regular sea-
breeze, and this, together with the heavy dews, tends
materially to mitigate the fierce temperature of a
climate seldom cooled by rain in twenty-five degrees
north latitude, on the verge of the tropic. Finally
the dry soil, the deposit of the river, and the *débris*
of the rocks, breeds none of that fearful miasma
which arises from the jungly swamps near the
embouchures of the Indus, and renders the Delta a
formidable rival to the Pontine Marshes.

But Kurrachee, like Aden, Muscat, Bushire, and
other similar places, though generally speaking
salubrious enough, has recurring crises of sickness,
suffering severely from the visitation of epidemics,
cholera, dysentery, and fever, and at such times
shows bills of mortality which shame even Sierra
Leone, celebrated as she justly is for her habit of
running up a long account of that nature..

I am afraid, sir, that something of the kind is in
the wind now. You recollect, when we returned
from afternoon service yesterday, my calling your
attention to the peculiar lurid tinge which overspread

---

* On the coast the thermometer would not rise higher than 90°
Fahrenheit; when at Hyderabad and Sukkur, it would be 110°.

the face of nature: perhaps, too, you have not forgotten the sensations of which you complained
during our evening walk. The air felt as if we
were standing upon the crater of Vesuvius on a
windless day; it was still and stagnant as if its powers
of motion had passed away; our lungs were parched
by the unwholesome unnatural heat, and our eye-
balls were scorched as if they had been exposed to
the burning rays of the mid-day sun. Our spirits
were more depressed even than we might have
expected them to be; we recognised a sinking of the
heart, a painful anxiety about nothing, and sundry
other symptoms which boded no good. A native
remarked to us that all the kites and birds of prey,
generally wheeling and hovering over the camp, had
disappeared, and he considered their departure
another by no means propitious omen. Finally, it
is the seventh year, and though you may not attach
much importance to such coincidence, I do.

This morning three stout fellows—privates in her
Majesty's — regiment, died of Asiatic cholera in its
most malignant doctor-baffling shape. The victims
were alive and well yesterday evening. By breakfast
time to-morrow, there will be a dozen in their graves
and a score or two in hospital.

Entre nous, the best thing we can do is to be off at once, sir. You have now every necessary for a long march—a bechoba, or poleless tent of Bengal, not Bombay * manufacture, with a single fly and two side-flaps, for your people to sleep under. Also an old Arab—a veteran hog-hunter, and a steady roadster—an Affghan yaboo, as they call that breed of short, stout, shaggy pony, a sandnee or dromedary for your own riding, and four baggage camels to carry your canvass home, and its furniture, table, and chair, canteen and crockery, couch, carpet, and chest of drawers. Your other animals are eight in number; " Pepper," a spiteful little terrier, the best possible body-guard during a march, a head servant, at once butler, footman, valet, and cook ; a boy, his *aide-de-camp*, two horsekeepers, a grass cutter, and a pair of camel drivers. We must take a washer-woman and certain unclean drudges between us.

There are two ways of getting to Gharra, the first station on the road to Hyderabad, one by water, the other by land. If, however, preferring the former, with a view to save trouble, we take a boat at Ghizree Bunder, the embarkation place, near " Clifton," we shall probably find ebb tide in the

---

* The former are as justly famous as the latter are despised. A Bengal tent will generally last out two Bombay ones.

creek, a desolating sun and a strong wind dead in our teeth. So we will make up our mind to start the servants directly, with orders to march upon Jemadar-Ka Landa,† the nearest stage, distant about thirteen miles from camp.

*   *   *

Our route lies eastward of Kurrachee, over the low hills, and the little desert where the dust storms love to wander. There is little remarkable in it, except that we are morally certain to lose the road — if such name can be given to the one in a thousand footpaths and hoof-tracks into which we happened to fall when we left the cantonment—so regularly every half-hour, that our journey will more than double its proper length.

That pole on the summit of the little hill we are now passing marks the spot where a celebrated Scindee, "Wildfire Dick," by name Fakirah, paid the last penalty of the law for murdering an English officer in cold blood. An old hyæna prowls about the spot, and the credulous natives believe him to be the cacodemon, whose foul influence impelled the freebooter to do so *unlucky* a deed.

Observe, every one we meet is in peaceful guise.

* The "Jemadar's Station;" so called from a native official, who many years ago built a mud tower near the village.

One of the first orders issued by the conqueror of Scinde was, that no man should carry weapons about his person. It was one of the old warrior's shrewd, wise, despotic, measures. Large bodies of armed men were thereby prevented from meeting to concert conspiracies, and quiet people saw with astonishment and admiration that the personal safety of the subject was become a public, not a private care. Many a Kurrachee-ite remembers the day when no man dared walk from the town to the Ram-Bagh, a distance of half a mile, without sword and shield, matchlock and dagger.

To show you what the value of human life was in those days :—Some fifteen years ago, a clan of Beloochies had wandered down from their native mountains, and had pitched their tents on the plain that lies to the north of the cantonment. It is related that on one occasion an old lady—a widow—sent forth her only son to collect a little "rhino" from any travellers he might chance to meet. She buckled on his sword like a Spartan mother, praying lustily the while, and followed with anxious eyes his lessening form, making it the object of many a heart-breathed benison.

It was the boy's maiden foray, and he started upon it with the determination not to disgrace the lengthy line of celebrated thieves, his ancestors. The first person he met was a Scindian, trudging along on foot, armed as usual, *cap-à-pié*, and carrying on his back an earthen pot-lid, the extent of his morning's purchases at the neighbouring market town.

To cry "stand and deliver!" was the work of a moment. As rapidly, too, the order was obeyed— a native of these plains seldom dared to bandy words or blows with an armed highlander.

The young Belooch secured the pot-lid.

But presently the dark idea of the maternal disappointment and disgust at the paltry nature of his virgin booty, and the danger of being disgracefully designated a "prigger of pot-lids," settled heavily upon the boy's sensitive mind. What was he to do? Suddenly a bright thought dispersed the gloomy forebodings. He cut the Scindian down, struck off his head, placed it upon the platter and carried it in triumph as a peshkash, or honorary offering, to his mamma.

"And hast thou really slain this Scindee dog for the sake of this pot-lid, two of which go for a farthing, my son?" anxiously inquired the venerable matron, with a beating heart.

"Wallah—by the Lord—I did, mother!"

"Then happy am I, among the daughters of the Belooch, and blessed be thou, my boy! and thy sons! and thy son's sons! for ever and ever!" quoth the widow, bursting into a crying fit of joy.

*　　　*　　　*　　　*

We, however, use the privilege of the ruling race, as our holsters show, not so much for the purpose of safety as with the object of impressing the natives with a sense of our national superiority. The only dangerous animal we are at all likely to meet with here is some native trooper's runaway jade. Remember, if you do see one charging us, with tail erect and head depressed, whinnying like the Fire King's steed, draw your revolver, and put him at once *hors de combat.*

Our first day's march is interesting in one point of view: during the whole morning's ride, we see not one inch of cultivated, though every second mile of it is culturable, ground. The road crosses a number of fiumaras, all sand at this season, and stretches over a succession of heavy shingles, bare rocks, and burning deserts, which would not be out of place in Bedouin land.

There is the Jemadar's station. It is a fair specimen of the village in southern Scinde: the component matter consists of a well, a few shops or

booths of matting, where vendors of grain, sweetmeats, vegetables, and clarified butter expose their
scanty stores, and a ragged line of huts, half mud,
half "rain-dropping wattles, where, in foul weather,
the tenant (like poor Paddy) can scarcely find a dry
part to repose his sky-baptised head," and where, in
summer season, the occupant, one would suppose, is
in constant imminent peril of sun-stroke and brain-
fever. Our tent is pitched upon a dwarf plain near
the road, our effects are scattered upon its withered
grass plat, and our people are loitering about the
bushes beyond, or squatting under the single tree,
in expectation of our arrival.

You dismount, somewhat stiffly. It is your first
ride after some months, and a long canter is apt to
produce temporary inconvenience. You will, doubtless, be better in the afternoon.

And now for breakfast—*à la Scindienne :* Bass
usurping the throne of Hyson, unleavened cakes of
wheaten flour, salt, and water, doing duty as
buttered toast, and a hot curry the succedaneum for
cold meat.

If there be anything of the wanderer in your
disposition, Mr. Bull, and I know there is, you will
soon like this style of life. The initiation is, of
course, an effort. After gliding over a railroad at

the rate of thirty-five miles per hour, you are disposed to grumble at our creeping pace on the line of march. At the halt, you miss your " comforts," your hotel, your newspaper, and your thousand unnecessary necessaries of civilised existence. One of your camels has fallen down and broken half your crockery—you need not turn up your eyes in despair; it is quite as easy to drink ale out of a tea-cup as a' tumbler. Your couch is a perfect wreck—never mind, we will make up another, in the shape of a wooden frame, listed along and across, with a hook at each corner, and secure it between two bullock trunks. Our servants, I hear, have been fighting, as Turks are said to do. This is a real annoyance: we must crush it in embryo, if we want to live in peace.

We summon the offenders. After the delay natural to the man, who expects no good to come of haste, appear Messieurs Rama and Govind, plaintiff and defendant.

" O sons of doggesses! What shameful work is this?"

"Sahib, is it by your order and direction that thy man smites me upon the lips with his slipper?" asks Rama, blubbering.

" Sahib, is it by your order and direction that

this man calls my mother naughty names, and tells
me that I eat corpses?" inquires Govind, fiercely.

We dismiss both parties, with a little counter
irritation applied by my tongue and boot to something more tangible than the part chafed by angry
words. Those fellows, both having reason, as they
imagine, to abuse us, will be on the best possible
terms before sunset, and they are not likely to
quarrel again soon, much less to annoy us with their
disputes.

The sea-breeze blows freshly here, and, after
breakfast, you will enjoy a nap exceedingly.

*   *   *   *

Now, Mr. Bull, I will tell you how I employed
my mind, whilst you were dozing away the forenoon.

Do you see that array of striped tents, those
scattered boxes, neglected bags, and heaps of camel
litters, in whose glaring shade repose some dozens
of long-bearded individuals, with huge conical caps
of lamb's wool, fierce eyes, thick beards, loud voices,
and a terrible habit of profane swearing?

They are Persians, escorting one of the prettiest
girls ever seen to her father's house, near Kurrachee.

The first thing which attracted my attention after
you went to sleep, was the appearance of a little
slave boy, who, when his fellow domestics addressed

themselves to the morning siesta, kept walking about the entrance of our tent, looking in at times, and taking every precaution to evade all eyes but mine. I awaited an opportunity, and called him up. He removed his slippers, salaamed, bending forward with his hand on his right thigh,* and then stood up to be catechised.

"Who art thou, son?"

"My name is Lallu—birth-place, Bushire."

"And what is thy employment?"

"I serve the Beebee, in the house of the great Sardar,†—A***a Khan."

"Indeed! thou art a wonderful youth. Dost thou like confectionery? Then take this rupee, go to the bazaar, and stuff thyself. If thou wishest to come here presently and chat awhile, there is no fear."

The little wretch—he scarcely numbers twelve summers—looked knowing as a boy in your city of infant phenomena; again bowed, shuffled on his slippers and departed, with a grin and a promise to return.

Then taking my pen and ink, I proceeded to indite the following *billet doux* upon a sheet of

---

* A very respectful style of salutation, called in Persia the "kurnish."
† A noble.

bright yellow note paper, the "correct thing" in this early stage of an *affaire* (*de cœur*), we will call it :—

"The rose-bud of my heart hath opened and bloomed under the rays of those sunny eyes, and the fine linen * of my soul receiveth with ecstasy the lustres which pour from that moon-like brow.   But, woe is me ! the garden lacketh its songster, and the simooms of desire have dispersed the frail mists of hope.   Such this servant (*i. e.* myself) knows to be his destiny ; as the poet sings—

> " ' Why, oh ! why, was such heavenly beauty given
>   To a stone from the flint rock's surface riven ? '

" Even so the hapless inditer of this lament remarketh that—

> " ' The diamond's throne is the pure red gold ;
>   Shall the almas † rest on the vile black mould ? '

"And he kisseth the shaft which the bow of Fate hath discharged at the bosom of his bliss.   And he looketh forward to the grave which is immediately to receive him and his miseries.   For haply thy foot may pass over his senseless clay ; the sweet

---

* This Oriental image may not be familiar to the English reader.   In Persian poetry, the stuff called karbas is supposed—why I know not—to be enamoured of the moon.

† The adamant or diamond.   The verses are Nizami's.

influence of thy presence may shed light over that dark abode."

Then after sealing this production with wax the same colour as the paper, I traced the following lines with an unsteady hand, in very crooked and heart-broken characters, upon the place where " Miss A—— " &c., &c., would have been.

> " The marks on this sheet are not the stains of smoke (*i. e.* ink),
> But the black pupils of my eyes dissolved by scalding tears;
> Ask of my heart what its fate is—it will tell thee
> That when tears are exhausted, its blood will begin to flow."

When the slave-boy reappeared we renewed our dialogue, and, after much affected hesitation, he proceeded to disclose further particulars. Etiquette forbad his mentioning the lady's name; on other subjects, however, the young Mercury was sufficiently communicative, and at last he departed with a promise to put the missive into the Beebee's hand when he could, and to report progress in the course of the afternoon.

*   *   *   *

Now, Mr. Bull, be asleep if you please! Lallu is sneaking about the tent again, and the presence of a " party " *en tiers* operates unfavourably on these occasions. Turn your face towards the tent wall, Sir!

" Well, son ? "

" I have laid the high letter before the Beebee."

" And what commands did the Beebee issue ? "

" Hich ! nothing "—

" Indeed ! "

—" Except that the Beebee wished to know if you are learned in physic, and have any European remedies with you."

" Take my prayers and compliments to the Beebee, and put in this petition, saying, That in half-an-hour I will lay before her ladyship what we men of medicine in Feringistan consider the Elixir of Life."—

" I scarcely know what to do. Perhaps, Sir, you do not diagnosticise the fair one's malady? A flask of curaçoa or noyau would cure it at once, but we have none with us. Brandy she will dislike, sherry she will find cool, and ale nauseous."

" I have it ! "

We did not neglect when at Kurrachee to lay in a little store of coarse gin, intended as a *bonne bouche* for the Scindes. See what ingenuity can effect ! I mix up a bottle of it with a pound of powdered white sugar, simmer over a slow fire, strain, flavour with an idea of Eau de Cologne, and turn out as dainty a dram, sweet and strong, as any liquor-loving Oriental queen could desire.

The boy is delivering the Elixir of Life, and a certain accompanying message from the Jalinus * of the age, viz., your humble servant, to his mistress. If you peep through that crevice in the tent wall you may catch sight of her.

Is she not a charming girl, with features carved in marble like a Greek's, the noble, thoughtful, Italian brow, eyes deep and lustrous as an Andalusian's, and the airy, graceful, kind of figure with which Mohammed, according to our poets, peopled his man's paradise?

How laggingly Time creeps on! When will it be evening? O that I could administer a kick to those little imps the Minutes that would send them bumping against one another, bow and stern, as the eight-oars in a rowing match on old Isis! I shall be admitted into the presence as a medico of distinguished fame, and you may accompany me to play propriety and to enlarge your ideas, sir.

*   *   *   *

Confusion! what are they doing?

The litters are being hoisted upon the camel's back and that grim senior, the Beebee's male duenna, has entered her tent!

O "my prescient soul!" The fair one comes

* Galen.

forth muffled and wrapped up; the beast, her dromedary, kneels; she mounts, turning her latticed *
face towards us; I hear a tiny giggle; she whispers
a word in the ear of the slave girl that sits beside
her; the auditor also laughs; they draw the litter
curtains; the camels start—

* Modest women, in Persia, when they leave the house, always wear the
burka.   See Chapter xiv.

CHAPTER V.

THE LEGEND OF BHAMBORA—SCINDIA DESERTA—THE FAREWELL ORDER OF A COMMANDER-IN-CHIEF AND THE CAMEL RIDER.

WE are now progressing towards Wuttajee, the second stage from Kurrachee, on the road of the Five Torrents—about which anon.

Wuttajee affords the unusual convenience of a caravanserai; a deserted mosque having been desecrated into utility. It will be better when re-roofed, but in the long mean time we can make ourselves comfortable enough, half exposed to the winds of heaven.

Native travellers you see, sir, have scribbled over the well-plastered walls, precisely as if they had been Englishmen; and our compatriots have not forgotten to write and scrape many a "GREEN" and a "BROWN" sprawlingly over the more modest signatures and the less striking inscriptions of their black fellow-subjects.

A few of the oriental compositions are amusing enough.

This one for instance:

> "Matters are come to a pretty pass, ye Moslems,
>   When Christian hounds eat pork and drink wine in the
>   Mosque!"

Some patriotic, probably "unemployed," * individual has recorded a burning wish in the following terms :—

> " O Shere Mahommed,† turn the reins of thy steed towards
>   Scinde,
>   And with one flash of thy brand consume ' Nupeer.' "

And a little below, fanatics, in their cups I should suppose, have been hard at work. One gentleman writes :—

> "A lac of evil curses light on the head of Umar ‡
>   The son of Khattab!"

Near which an orthodox Moslem has thus noted his violent detestation of such a schismatical, heretical, and damnable sentiment :—

> " O, base-born one, mayst thou die a hateful death,
>   And may dogs make a divan of thy tomb!"

This, you may observe, Mr. Bull, is the oriental

---

* "Employment," in this country, means a salary from government.

† The only Ameer in Scinde who showed courage or conduct in attacking or resisting us.

‡ The second Caliph or successor to Mohammed: he is always cursed by the Shieh sect.

way of doing the NO POPERY and the BAD END
TO THE POPE, which, at periods of excitement,
you are fond of seeing chalked upon your walls and
pavements at home and in the sister island.

    *   *   *   *

From Wuttajee to Gharra this morning—a plain
such as Scinde only can display. I feel almost
disposed to point out the marks of the old coast, and
to lecture you upon the " geology and extinct fishes "
of the country. However, that hill, a few hundred
yards off the road, rising abruptly on one side from
the sandy flat that skirts the neighbouring creek,
and on the other sinking gradually into the broken,
bushy, rocky ground behind it, will supply us with
half an hour's " story-telling," certainly much more
rational, and probably a little more amusing.

Bhambora—some identify it with the ancient em-
porium Barbarika—is supposed by the natives to be
the most ancient sea-port in Scinde. Nothing of its
former state now remains but the foundations of
houses, bastions, and walls, and the ghostly romances
which haunt the deserted hill-top.

Tradition asserts, that the city and its citizens
were all swallowed up in one night because of the
prodigious wickedness of the ruler Dilu Rahi, who
had set his mind upon compelling the fair dame of a

Moslem convert to break a certain commandment.
It is still a celebrated locality in this part of the
world on account of the following bit of rude
poetry which the bards and minstrels have associated
with it:—

In the days when Islam began to take firm root
in Scinde, and like the glorious Tuba* of Paradise,
to afford goodly fruit and sweet perfume and grateful
shade to the erring souls that wandered over the
Saharas of transgression, worshiping wood, stone
and metals, the wife of a Brahmin, at Tattah, on
the Indus, bare him a daughter. It was a lovely
child in face and form, but the astrologers, having
consulted their books, declared her fate was to become
a Muslimah,† to marry a foreigner, and to disgrace
her family. Determined to avert this prodigious evil
from themselves, the parents procured a coffer, placed
the babe in it with a rich bracelet, and committed
her to the safeguard of the sacred stream. Mother,
as the poet sings, never nursed Sassooee; the wild
waves cradled her on their rough bosom, and the
wilder winds howled her lullaby.

By the decree of destiny,—and who can escape it?
—the ark floated down to Bhambora, in those days a
flourishing city with glittering spires and proud

---

* The Tuba is a wonderful tree in Mohammed's heaven.
† A she-moslem.

palaces, whose walls towered majestic as monarchs over the surrounding country, and whose gardens lay beautiful as the plains which houris tread.

A washerman, who was exercising his craft on the bank of the Indus, drew out the coffer, and, astonished at the sight of its beautiful contents, called to the by-standers, his " disciples," " See, O ye men, the tricks of the world; to the childless, a child is borne by the river ! "

After the lapse of years, the fair Sassooee became the boast and the beauty of Bhambora. No scimitar ever dealt more deadly wounds than did the curve of her eyebrow; no shaft pierced deeper into man's heart than the lashes that defended her lovely orbs; her brow shone dazzlingly as the light of day, and her hair gloomed deeply as the midnight murks. Speaking in English, she was a very pretty girl, and made a considerable sensation in (female) society.

As the fair one was sitting with her companions, spinning at the window of her atan, a travelling trader happened to pass by. The young ladies, admiring his handsome appearance, called him in,— he was a Hindoo, so they were not under apprehension of his regards,—and began a conversation consisting of coquetry and curiosity in equal parts. After

* The Atan in Scinde is the Gynæceum, or ladies' apartment

many questions and answers, they found out that he was servant of Ari, the Beloch chief, whose city was Kech, in the province of Mekran. Moreover, the conscientious Babiho, when highly complimented upon the subject of his comeliness, declared himself an ifrit,* (a fright as we say), in comparison with his young master—Punhu Khan.

Forthwith the fire of love arose from the fuel of Sassooee's heart; for, as saith the wise man,

"Ofttimes the ear loveth before the eye."

And surrendering herself to the tyrant with amiable *abandon*, she indited, or caused to be indited, a note of invitation to her unseen flame, and sent him a handsome jacket,—a delicate hint, I presume, to come dressed like a gentleman.

Punhu, by the subtlety of Babiho, his father's bagsman, escaping the paternal surveillance, which is described to be even stricter than that of the French police, visited the fair Sassooee, loved her, and lived in her adopted parents' house under the humble disguise of a washerman, till he earned his prize, and married his mistress. A world of happi-

---

* The Arabic word is ifrít, an iambic, according to our ideas. The Muse of Anglo-Eastern poetry has changed it to afrit, and made it, moreover, a trochee.

ness now lay before the pair, who prepared themselves for a charming cruise, *en tête-à-tête*, down the stream of days. But upon the Indus, as elsewhere, (alas!) there is a snagg called Circumstance upon which the frail barque of Love is sorely apt to strike.

It is related, that when Ari, the proud old Beloch, heard of his Benjamin's abominable conduct, he tore off his turban, and dashed it to the ground, scattered ashes upon his vestments, rent his skirts, spoiled his shirt-front, and positively refused to wash. Moreover, not content with thus benefiting his tailor, he sent at least two dozen of his stalwart sons to fetch the fugitive home; and—though this is a mere conjecture on my part—I doubt not that he occupied himself sedulously during their absence in preparing a stout rod for the benefit of the young gentleman's corduroys. The hard-hearted fraternity, furious at the idea of a Beloch's degrading himself to take in foul linen, hastened to Bhambora, and, in no wise appeased by their sister-in-law's beauty, kindness, hospitality, and skill in cookery, succeeded, partly by force and partly by stratagem, in carrying off Punhu very drunk upon the back of a high trotting dromedary.

Who can describe Sassooee's grief, when awaking at dawn she opens her lovely eyes, and looks lovingly and finds no beloved husband by her side? She does not faint—Scindee women still have so much to learn!—but she shrieks and wrings her hands, and weeps rainy tears thick as the drops that patter upon the hills over which her lover is being borne. The fresh footprints upon the sand reveal the "horrid truth," and the lady feels that for her there is left but one course—pursuit.

Her "poor mother" reminds her of her duties—she heeds not the maternal words; her companions prognosticate—as friends are so fond of doing—a million certain disasters, concluding with murder and sudden death.

> "Go not forth to the wild, where snakes lurk,
>   Where wolves and bears sit in ambush for the wayfarer,
>   Where fierce hornets buzz."—&c. &c. &c.

She merely forbids them to accompany her—they never offered to do so, be it observed—in these moving words:—

> "Follow me not, ye damsels and dames,
>   Lest haply, when dying of thirst, ye curse my husband!"

And starts on foot, alone, without kit or provender, for a two hundred mile march, across a dreadful desert.

What a barbarous land it must be that can dream of producing such a woman; or rather, what a terrible state of society it is that can read so improbable an incident, and not reject it, and not call the author " loon ! "

The road of the Five Torrents (we travelled over it yesterday, Mr. Bull,) was, in those days, a waste of waters : the fair one dried them up by the fervency of her prayers, and, by similar efficacious means, caused the drainage of the hills to flow down ready-scooped-out channels. I gallop hurriedly over the wide field of description—the novelty of the lady's feelings, the peculiarities of her ejaculations, the variety of her apostrophes, and the praiseworthy intensity of her perseverance, in spite of sun, simoon, fatigue, and sore feet—and, cramming my Pegasus at the fence of conclusion, hasten to be in at the death.

Sassooee presently reached the Pubb mountains, where, faint with thirst, she applied to a goatherd for a draught of milk. Now Fate had so disposed it that this wretch, who deserves the name, being described as a perfect Caliban in hideous appearance, had been told by the old Sycorax, his mama, that a beautiful bride would about that time meet him in the wild. Seeing the fair wanderer, he at once determined that she was the proper person, and forthwith began a display of affection and gallantry, to say the least of it, decidedly inconvenient under the circumstances. At length the unfortunate one,

driven to despair, again petitioned to Heaven to preserve her honour, which it did by the rough and
ready expedient, commonly manifested in Scinde, of
causing her to sink bodily beneath the yawning
ground.   Then Caliban, convinced that there was
some mistake about the matter, fell, like a monster
as he was, to howling over his wickedness, and then
to piling up a mound of stones—a couthless tribute
to departed purity and loveliness.

As usually happens, or is made to happen in such
cases, Punhu, who had slipped away from the grim
fraternity, arrived at the identical spot of his wife's
vivi-sepulture exactly five minutes after the monu-
ment had been erected.   Suddenly he hears a voice
from below—he stands—he listens :—

> " Enter boldly, my Punhu ; think not to find a narrow bed.*
> Here gardens bloom, and flowers shed sweetest savour ;
> Here are fruits, and shades, and cooling streams,
> And the Prophet's light pours through our abode,
> Banishing from its limits death and decay."

Can he refuse to comply with the modest request ?
Ah no !—

> " Not such his faith, not such his love."

---

* These lines contain the popular superstitions upon the subject of individuals that die in the valour of sanctity. Their graves are wide and
light, rather pleasant places than otherwise, and their bodies are not regularly dead and liable to decay like those of ordinary mortals. No true
Moslem doubts for a moment that his Prophet's corpse, were the tomb
opened, would appear exactly as it did in life.

He prayed and was swallowed up, and became a saint accordingly.

*   *   *   *

Look at that unhappy hole—it is Gharra.

The dirty heap of mud and mat hovels that forms the native village is built upon a mound, the *débris* of former Gharras, close to a creek which may or may not have been the "western outlet of the Indus in Alexander's time." All around it lies a—

"windy sea of land :"--

salt, flat, barren rock and sandy plain, where eternal sea gales blow up and blow down a succession of hillocks—warts upon the foul face of the landscape —stretching far, far away, in all the regular irregularity of desolation.

You see the cantonment with its falling brick lines outside, and its tattered thatched roofs peeping from the inside of a tall dense hedge of bright green milk bush. Upon that place I intend to hang a tale, Mr. Bull—a quiet little bit of egotism which might, but probably will not, edify or instruct you.

Some years ago when my corps was ordered up to young Egypt, we were sent to relieve a regiment about to quit Gharra. Our predecessors had not built barracks or bungalows, because they knew that their time of field-service in Scinde was ended. But we, who had four or five years of it in prospect, found ourselves in a different position.

In this part of the Unhappy Valley, sir, the summer heat often reaches 115°; for a tent add perhaps 10°.

Now 125° of Fahrenheit, lasting, mind you, for months together, is exceedingly likely to hurry and hustle one half-roasted to one's hot grave. However strong a man may be, his eyes burn, his ears sing, and his brain turns dizzy under the infliction: sleepless, appetiteless, spiritless, and half speechless, he can scarcely be said to live: at the end of the season, if he reaches it, looking at his face you would pronounce him to be in a "galloping consumption."

Build or burn, then, was our dilemma. The only chance of saving health—a soldier's all in all—was to house ourselves. But there lay the difficulty.

Let me tell you, sir, that it requires no little prudence and determination for a subaltern to live upon his pay :* setting aside the not unimportant consideration that if in these regions one lives only to live within one's means, one is commonly likely to be loved by the gods and to die young. He must have no expensive tastes; such as a hanker-

* This applies only to Scinde and the dearer parts of the three Presidencies.

ing for neatness of house and furniture, or high ideas of hospitality; he must have no ambition to distinguish himself as a sportsman, a linguist, a traveller, or a "good fellow;" he must rest content in that happy obscurity, which we are told is as excellent for man as for the ignoble part of creation. If he be a married man I defy him to do it, unless at least he can make up his mind to see his wife become a confirmed invalid, and his children pining away to spectres for want of a cold climate. Even as a bachelor, to keep out of debt he must be favoured by circumstances as well as by nature. Now we were not. The regiment had been travelling hundreds of miles, and expected a journey of as many more with all the expensive consequences of carriage and marching mess-bills.* And yet we found it necessary to expend two or three months' prospective pay upon brick and mortar.

Had we applied to the financial department at home, the train of reasoning would have been—

"That boy gets £20 a month: humph! 12 times 20 make 240: humph! Ah, it's always the way with these fellows in India—"

And the inevitable *ergo*.

* Expensive things, as the members of a mess have to pay for losses and breakage.

—"*I* wont encourage his extravagance."

For, you know, Mr. Bull, many a papa who makes a liberal allowance to a son in one of H.M.'s regiments, would pooh-pooh at the idea of sending a farthing per annum to one in the Company's service.

The gist of which is this :—It might be desired that high authorities when issuing their edicts to the Indian army, would be generous enough to be a little more considerate, a trifle more just. You are led, sir, to suppose, though not told to believe, that we exult in debt : the effects of our extravagance are skilfully deployed into line before your eyes, whilst the many unavoidable causes of our expenditure are as skilfully close columned and huddled up into one corner of the rhetorical field.

I own that rigid economy is not the virtue of Indians. But can you fairly expect it to be? In this country many things, horses for instance, are necessaries; at home they would be luxuries. Then there is always some amount of recklessness in the profession of arms. Men are separated from family and friends, and made to feel that separation too. Letters, which during the first year of expatriation arrived regularly each mail, gradually diminish in number, shrink in size, cease altogether. They know that when they return home their relations will think and find them *de trop*—the average heart cannot stand up against ten years thorough separation—that their friends will have ceased to care for them, that their acquaintances will have clean forgotten them. Existence, too, in India is precarious: who can tell how soon a fever or a bullet may send him to the jackals? Consequently we are, perhaps, a little over anxious to "live whilst we may."

Such is our apology for want of thrift.

But it is not unnecessary to instruct us, that a man who deprives his servants of their wages to give champagne tiffins to his friends, is not acting like an officer or a gentleman; we are by no means grateful for such simple commentaries upon the code of honour, and, to speak plain truth, we are somewhat indignant to see that the information is deemed information by one usually so well informed as is our informer.

But what is the use of all this? You, Mr. Bull, have old, long-cherished ideas of our extravagant style of life—the memories of the last century floating in your head—and you see with delight the daring hand outstretched in might to tear up the root of the evil Bosh! Were he that chatteth with you Lt.-Gen. Sir R. Burton, G.C.B., instead of

being a small lieutenant, then might he have some
hope of an occasional cheer from you, to enliven his
squabble with a brother veteran. Then might he,
it is believed, have some little chance of winning
the day, however doughty in the cacoethes of scribble,
however skilful in the use of oxymoron or antithesis,
however fond of the *ad captandum*, and however suc-
cessful in writing pointedly, not to the point, well
but not wisely, that same brother veteran may be.

But now, sir, I feel myself over-matched—weight
is against me—it is " no go." Excuse the folly of
tilting at a windmill strong in the breath of popular
opinion and—let us order the camels.

*   *   *   *

You had better mount your dromedary this morning for the first time. You need not be afraid of
approaching him, as he is a particularly quiet beast;
only do not get into the habit of walking carelessly
within reach of camels' tusks and hind legs. The
kick is an awful one, so is the bite : the brutes hold
like bull dogs, and with the purchase afforded by
their long pliable necks they can twist your arm off
in a minute.

Before throwing your leg over the framework of
wood, padded and covered with a thickly quilted
gaudy-coloured silk cushion, acting saddle, shake

the bells that garnish your animal's necklace of
blue beads, a talisman against the *mal occhio*, and
give him a bit of biscuit. If you startle him at first
when mounting him, he is very apt to get into a
habit of converting his squatting into a standing
position, with a suddenness by no means pleasant.
There, you are on now. Hold his nose-string
lightly; give him his head, and after once putting
him in the right path, let him do what he pleases.

My first ride was not such a pleasant one as yours
will be, partly my own fault for mounting a baggage
camel. After considerable difficulty in getting on
the roaring, yelling beast, it became palpably necessary to draw my sword and prick his nose each
time it crept round diagreeably near my boot. Finding his efforts to bite me unavailing, he changed
tactics, and made a point of dashing under every
low thorn tree, as close to the trunk as possible, in
the hope of rubbing his rider off. This exercise he
would vary by occasionally standing still for half an
hour, in spite of all the persuasive arguments in the
shape of heels, whip, and rapier, with which I plied
his stubborn sides. Then he would rush forward, as
if momentarily making up his mind to be good.
At last he settled upon the plan of running away;
arched his long neck till his head was almost in

contact with mine, and in this position indulged in a canter, which felt exactly like the pace of a horse taking a five-barred gate every second stride.

Fortunately for me the road was perfectly level.

Presently snap went the nose-string. My amiable *monture* shook his head once or twice, snorted a little blood from his nostrils, slackened his speed, executed a *demi-volte,* and turned deliberately toward the nearest jungle.

Seeing a swamp before us, and knowing that a certain "spill" was in prospect—these beasts always tumble down and often split their stomachs on slippery mud—I deliberated for a moment whether I should try to chop the fellow's head open, or jump off his back, risking the consequences, or keep my seat till it became no longer tenable. And my mind was still in doubt when he released it by sliding two or three yards through the slimy mire, and by falling plump upon his sounding side.

I did not mount that animal again.

Somehow or other the Arabs' superstition about the camel is not without a sure foundation; they assure you that no man was ever killed by a fall from these tall beasts, whereas a little nag has lost many a life. Certainly I have seen some furious "rolls," and have myself been dismounted about a dozen times, yet not even a trifling accident occurred.

Should, however, your dromedary when trotting high at the rate of ten or eleven miles the hour, happen to plant his foot upon the stump of a tree, or to catch in a bandycoot's hole, it might so be that after a flight of a few yards you would reach *terra firma* with an impetus calculated to put the Arabs' proverb out of joint. Still remember there is a knack in falling, as in most other things. You may let a corpse drop from a height of thirty feet without breaking the smallest bone, and a drunken man, after tumbling from the gallery of a theatre, will rise and perhaps walk quietly home. So, also, you may roll off your camel with as little injury as a sack of wheat would incur, if you only have the presence of mind not to catalepse your members. Let every limb be lax and bending: it is by the strong muscles in a state of convulsive rigidity that compound fractures are caused.

The " Ship of the Desert " is the reindeer of the Scindians—an animal of many uses. They drink the milk: it tastes rather salt and thin at first, but the palate soon becomes accustomed to it; they make butter of it, and employ it in confectionary. The flesh of the camel colt is considered a kind of religious meat: it is infinitely superior to horseflesh, and reminds one not a little of coarse veal.

Thousands of Scindians live by breeding camels; in the districts where tamarisk and mimosa abound, the country is covered with their straggling herds, and some tribes, the Jats, for instance, live by practising farriery, if I may so call it. There are about fifteen races peculiar to the ·province; the best, however, are imported. The small, stout, shaggy animals—regular camel-ponies—come from Muskat and Mekran : the tall large white dromedaries from Jesulmere; the dark, short-legged, two-humped beast, the cart-horse of the species, from Persia and Bokhara. Under the native princes this branch of the import trade was much encouraged, and 50*l.* was not an unusual price for a noted Sandni.*

These animals cannot easily be taught to pull;† for carrying burdens, however, they are invaluable. They will travel for months together if laden lightly, say up to two hundred and fifty pounds, if allowed sufficient time to forage for their scanty food in the woods,‡ and never halted, as well as never hurried on

---

* A riding or blood-camel; a dromedary.

† In the Bengal presidency they have been trained to draw guns, and did excellent service in the N. W. parts of India, where the deep and sandy roads punished the artillery horses and bullocks most severely.

‡ On long journeys, it is usual to give each camel a pound of barley

the line of march. Our ruinous losses in commissariat camel-flesh have mainly been occasioned by
neglecting these precautions. To which may be
added our utter ignorance of the animal's many and
various diseases. On one occasion I saw a friend
administer a bottle of Cognac to a favourite Sandni
by way of curing a stomach-ache. The dose did so
most effectually, for the dosed died, drunk as drunk
could be, half-an-hour afterwards.

A well-trained dromedary's trot is by no means
disagreeable, any other pace feels as if you were
riding two animals at once.* In this province they
are never made to canter or gallop, as in Arabia and
Belochistan.

*   ⌢   ⌢   *

That half-deserted ruinous-looking village is

---

per diem. The grain is reduced to flour, kneaded with water, and made
into lumps, which are thrust down the brute's throat. The Persians call
it "*Nawaleh.*" When a very severe march is in prospect, they sometimes add a little intoxicating hemp, mixed with clarified butter.

* In a wild country, where a pocket-compass or a sextant is the only
instrument a traveller can safely use, the camel acts admirably as a per_
ambulator. The result of the many observations I made was, that the
animal when treading on level ground, not rough or stony, takes one step,
exactly equal to a yard, per second ; that is to say, 3600 yards, or two
miles and eighty yards per hour. This calculation agrees precisely with
Volney's. Burnes estimates 3700 yards, when marching over soft and
sandy soils. This is probably correct ; but I doubt that a string of camels
generally moves so fast as 3833 yards per hour, as in one part of his Travels
he computes them to do.

Goujah. It offers an old mud mosque for the convenience of travellers, but as the place has been full
of natives, and consequently, will be in the last state
of filth, I have had the tents pitched under that cool-
looking fragrant mango-tope.* It also contains a
celebrated Sayyid, a gentleman of the blood holy,
very sacred and very unapproachable.

You are ruminating upon an object which fed
your fancy a little, and startled your mind a trifle this
morning's ride—a strange symbol of strange civilisation—a time-honoured relic of antiquity, which,
wonderful to say, maintains in your establishment
(long may it do so!), much of its ancient state
—Madam Britannia's "hieroglyphic state-machine"
and favourite three-legged *monture*—the gibbet. This
one had room to accommodate several, you may have
observed; it was made for a number of Belooch
banditti, who, some years ago, cut a Parsee's throat in
consideration of his brandy and pickled onions. I
own it has a peculiar appearance amidst these scenes,
a look which suggests a how-the-deuce-did-you-
come-here? phase of Inquisitiveness, and a general
impressiveness which is not easily rubbed out from
the page of recollection.

* *Tope* is the Anglo-Indian name for a tuft of trees, particularly
mangoes.

CHAPTER VI.

TATTAH AND ITS HOLY HILL.

NUGUR TATTAH—*the* city, as it is called *par excellence*, is a place of many lions. For the convenience of sight-seeing we will deposit our Penates on the banks of the bit of water which skirts the foot of the Mekli hills, about a mile south-east of the town. We now stand seventy miles from Kurrachee, near the apex of the Delta, on the western bank of the Indus, out of the first Desert.

The ancient capital of Lower Scinde is indeed fallen from its high estate. The population, once two hundred and eighty thousand, has diminished to five thousand; its thirty miles circumference has shrunk to ten; of its five thousand looms, which produced the shawls and silken stuffs * celebrated throughout Central Asia, scarcely remains a dozen;

---

* Generally silk and cotton mixed ; sometimes silk and gold. They are called *lung*, or waistcloths, and are supposed to be the *Zonœ* of the Periplus.

and of its four hundred colleges, not one is now in existence. The Mosque of Aurungzeb, with its towering walls and huge arches, still stands to show the ancient munificence of the Mogul viceroys, but all around it, far and near, is a squalid congeries of ruined or half-ruined habitations. Some of the streets are nearly blocked up by the masses of unbaked brick, which are allowed to moulder where they tumble, and in many quarters natural squares have been formed by the simple process of a heap of houses sinking to the ground. Each inundation sweeps away part of the suburbs exposed to its violence, and the rising places, such as Kurrachee and Hyderabad, every year draw off a portion of the wretched-looking population.

 *   *   *   т   .

We might as well dine at the Travellers' Bungalow to-day. Not that the old Portuguese " messman," as he calls himself, is likely to rival Verrey. But the building—the Company's old Factory*—is a curious one, it contains a large' court-yard and the upper story of rooms that looks into the quadrangle

---

* In A.D. 1758, Ghulam Shah, a prince of the Kalora dynasty, that then ruled the province, granted the Honourable East India Company permission to establish a factory in his dominions, with a view to the encouragement of trade between India and Scinde. This commercial connection was rudely broken off by Sarfaraz Khan Kalora, in 1775.

is surrounded by a wooden gallery which gives the building no small resemblance to an antiquated English inn. The chambers are large and high; many of them are in a ruinous condition, with huge holes in the threatening floors and ceilings. A long flight of steps leads to a flat roof of cement, whence we may chance to see some amusing scenes. The Scindians, Mr. Bull, sleep upon the roofs of their houses, and use them for a rich variety of domestic purposes.

Look! there is a party of young ladies enjoyin their favourite game with the Kheno;* their heads are bare and their muslin chemises are not of the most decorous cut; they run about, shout and push one another in their excitement, exactly like a bevy of English hoydens.

A little beyond, a busy housewife is spreading the night's resting-place—a couch as unartificial as could be desired, being nothing but a four-legged frame-work of wood, like your tent bedstead, with fine cords instead of tape, covered with the usual quilt.

There you see a little group, sitting at prayers upon a rug: the "head of the house," that venerable old gentleman with the long white beard, is teaching

* The ball.

his children to chaunt the Koran. It is a very devotional spectacle, and the voices of the juniors are soft and pleasing. You need not fear to distract their attention; not one of the party understands more than a parrot would do of what is being thus gravely repeated, so they can stare at us without disturbing their minds.

You look curiously at that whitish object which catches your eye in the deepening shades of eve. That is a Scindee performing his ablutions *in purissimis naturalibus*—a custom in these regions.

We must leave our eyrie. I see a pair of fiery eyes fiercely glaring at our inquiring countenances. There is nothing this people hate so much as to be overlooked; it is considered an outrageous violation of the sanctity of their domestic castles: we might as well humour them this once, as it grows dark, and it is time to return to our tents.

A word in your ear, Mr. Bull. If that little boy with the long hair down his shoulders—you recollect remarking him when we entered the bungalow?—comes up to you, asking you if you want anything, give him, or pretend to give him, a touch of your horsewhip. He is touter-general for the Kanyaris or dancing-girls: as you are a married man, and a *pater-familiás*, with a character, I cannot allow you a Nautch at a place so disreputable as Tattah is.

* * *

The cool of the morning will be a good time for visiting Kullian Kot, a ruin about a mile and a half south of Tattah. We ride along the skirt of the Mekli hills a couple of miles or so, through stubbles every stalk of which is as thick as an elderly gentleman's walking cane. The blithe "clock-clock" of the black partridge resounds from the neighbouring brakes; the *tittara* * rise in coveys from the pathway; every now and then, a timid hare, scarcely bigger than a small tom-cat, flies from our approach; or a fat jackal, returning from making a night of it, stands to look at us cunningly and officiously, as if he were the spy of the animal creation.

Kullian Kot was whilome a place of great fame. Our fellow-countrymen describe it as an immense camp, said to be the work of Alexander the Great. The people have a tradition that it is the feat of fairy hands: its name is Sanscrit, † and its appearance denotes that it was the erection of an age

* Grey partridge.
† "Fort Prosperous." Sir A. Burnes and Lieut. Wood incorrectly write and translate it *Kullan Kot*, the "Large Fort." Its Moslem name was *Toghlakabad*.

F 3

anterior to the general use of gunpowder—the round towers, of mud, revêted with kiln-burnt brick, which break the line of the outer curtain, are, you see, within easy bow-shot of one another. The *enceinte* contains a vast *terre pleine* of parallelo-grammical form, in obtaining earth for which the large tank below the ruins was probably excavated. Within the masses of masonry, many of which, shaken by time or earthquakes, have fallen into fantastic shapes resembling at a distance huge red rocks, there is Scindian desolation : a hard surface of dry kahgil—the mixture of clay and chopped straw used as plaster in this part of the world—thickly sown with bits of vitrified brick and tile, a broken wall or two, and a domed tomb converted by the pigeons into a dovecot : by these things we know that man has been there.

Riding along the crest of the hill, towards our tents, we pass over the spot where some unhappy Regiments * were stationed a few years ago. Every scrap of building has disappeared : in Lower Scinde such materials, especially wood, are too precious to

* The 22d and 26th Regiments, Bo. N. I., were stationed at Tattah when we first occupied the country. After a few months, they were quite disorganised, and nearly destroyed, by the fatal miasma of the plains. One of these unfortunate corps had 1576 cases treated in hospital between August and January, in the same year.

continue long unappropriated. But we can trace the foundations of the houses, and the ditches that surrounded them; probably they will last out the century. There is so little rain, that it takes many a season to obliterate deep marks from the hard, gravelly soil.

And now for the great lion of Tattah.

The "cities of the dead," I may observe, are the only populous places in Young Egypt. Many of the principal settlements must contain their hundreds of thousands. The reason is, that the people, being divided into clans, are fond of burying their relations together, as thereby the departed souls have the benefit of "spiritual confabulation," and the survivors have no difficulty to find out the grave over which they wish to perform such religious exercises as chaunting the Koran or reciting supererogatory prayers.

But this spot, as the first *coup d'œil* must convince you, is one of peculiar sanctity. Jam Tamachi —about whom presently—by order of a distinguished saint, built a mosque upon the hills, called them Mekli,* and directed that from that time forward this should be the holy *locale* of sepulture, in

* Properly written *Makkali,* " Mecca-like ;" in high degree of local virtue.

supersession of Pir Puttah on the Bhagar Creek, formerly the pet *Père la Chaise* of defunct Scindians.

Presently another distinguished saint, Miyan Maluk, discovered by the following peculiar test, that the Mekli hills had, in the olden time, been honoured by the revered presence of Hasan and Husain, the grandsons of Mohammed. An ignorant goatherd was in the habit of driving his flock over the rocks, and he observed, every day with increasing astonishment, that the animals studiously avoided planting hoof upon a certain place. The next thing in due order was a vision which the seer did not quite understand, but which when communicated by him to two learned and pious gentlemen, caused them to perform their orisons with such fervour, that neither they nor others could question the preternatural nature and origin of the "unction." They marked out the spot with stones; a governor of Tattah walled it round, another built a grand dome over it, and thus it gradually rose to the dizziest height of sanctity.

Great men hastened to be buried on the Mekli hills; saints and santons to the number of three thousand*—seventy-four of them immortal names in

---

* It is calculated that this burial-ground contains, in its six square miles, not less than a million of tombs. In Moslem countries, ancient graves are not re-opened, to admit fresh comers.

Scindian story, but very uninteresting ones to you, Mr. Bull—there depositing their venerable clay, increased its value as a cemetery to a prodigious extent. Like one Kevin who obtained from Heaven that all buried within the compass of the Seven Churches shall be saved on the day of judgment, their Moslem holinesses got permission to carry off when they rise again, the bit of hill bodily, contents and all, to be deposited in the courts of Paradise. No wonder that it was and is considered a luxury to be inhumed in such a locality; no wonder that people were and are made to pay for it!

From a distance the effect of the scene is imposing. The summit of the rocky ridge that looks towards the city of Tattah is crowned by an immense Eedgah*—a long wall with a low flight of steps leading to the central niche where the preacher stands, and tall slender minarets of elegant form springing from either extremity. Behind it is an infinite variety of mausolea and sepulchres, many reduced to ruins by the earthquake's shock, many crumbling to decay beneath the touch of time, a few and but very few preserved by the pious hands of descendants and disciples. Vaulted domes, arches,

---

* The name given to a place of worship, where public prayers are recited on the two great festivals, called the *Eed*.

and towers; porticos, gateways, and vast colonnades,
rise in apparently endless succession above shapeless
mounds of ruins, whose forms no ivy invests with its
green winding sheet,—heaps of stone naked, desolate, and unaltered, as on the day when they sank to
earth; here and there a tuft of parched up grass and
a thorny tree bowed by the winds and bare of leaves,
serving to communicate additional desolation to the
desolate spectacle.   Many of the edifices—the tombs
of chieftains and sayyids—must have been the
labour of years and years.   In some the cupola is
surrounded by a ring of smaller domes with a single
or a double colonnade, enclosing a gallery and platform, broken by pointed arches in each of the four
fronts; others are girt by lofty stone walls, forming
square court-yards, with entrance gates leading to
the different doorways.   Some consist of heavy
marble canopies supported by fantastic columns, and
sheltering a line of parallel tombstones; and many
are built of coloured and glazed Dutch tile and
brick,* with more the appearance of pleasure-houses

---

* Which, by-the-by, might rival those of old Rome.   No chiselled
stone could have a sharper edge, or a more accurate form.   So carefully is
each brick mixed and burned, that it rings as if of metal, and breaks
almost as clean as glass.   When stained and glazed, they look like
enamel: nothing can be richer than the appearance of the inscriptions, in
large white letters upon a dark purple ground.   They were, probably,

than mansions of the dead, adding a 'singularity to the general aspect of monotonous melancholy. Whilst upon all pours down the gay radiance of an Eastern sun, and the azure reflection of a cloudless sky, contrasting its hues of undying brightness with the transitory memorials of earthly splendour, tritely yet how impressively.

We pass over the hill. Every now and then some strolling fakir, grim as the ruins amidst which he stalks, frowns at the intrusion of the stranger, or a pariah dog barks as we approach, and then flies frightened by the echoed sound of his own voice. If we enter a mausoleum, the noise of our footsteps returned by the hollow ground, disturbs the hundred tenants of the porticos, the niches, and the projections of the domes.

A closer inspection is by no means favourable to the view. There is a satiating minuteness in the details of decoration with which the tombs are covered; in the largest and most magnificent, every stone of the edifice itself, its walls and its gates, is elaborately carved in relief. Your eye rejects the profuseness of square and circle, spiral and curve, diamond and scroll-work, flowers, border-pattern

made by Persian bricklayers, who are celebrated throughout the East for their skill in this craft.

and quotations from the Koran, in characters whose sole beauty is illegibility. In vain you look for a straight line in any building; the architects were not sufficiently skilful to succeed in the simplicities , of art. As a late traveller justly observes, the effect of the *tout ensemble* is gaudy, and there is that " appearance of tinsel tawdriness which results from injudicious over-ornament."

In these countries very little of " the history of these people is to be learned from their sepulchres," and the Moslems want the mania of epitaph and inscription which as often render our Christian monuments the means of mirth as of melancholy. Here the date of the " debt having been duly paid," sometimes a turban or a name, and rarely a verse from Holy Writ, or a Persian couplet, are the scanty scraps of information concerning the venerable defunct afforded to the anxious inquirer. That long tombstone of white alabaster under the bold cupola lined with blue and varnished tiles painted with flowers and arabesques so as to resemble the richest porcelain, is an exception to the general dulness and bears rather a pretty idea:

" Weeping thou didst enter this world of woe,
　Smiling thou departedst to that land of joy ! "

This is the mausoleum of a sayyid who, wonderful

to relate, is said to have been a cazee—a judge—and yet an honest man. He died in the odour of sanctity, literally as well as figuratively, amidst an overpowering aroma of musk from the apothecæ of Paradise. If you have any little pain flying about you, Mr. Bull, such as a twinge in the side or a slight abrasure of the skin, now is your time—rub it against the alabaster, with faith, mind, and you will assuredly recover. You see one of the great advantages of having holy places close at hand; where hospitals and surgeries do not abound, as here, they are quite *impayables*.

You may wish to know what supernatural and preternatural powers are attributed to the saints of Scinde. I offer you a *resumé* of the miracles which most commonly edify the mind and confirm the belief of the Faithful.

Causing the birth of children, especially in cases when the ages of the parents render prolificity a physical impossibility. Also on occasions of ingratitude being shown by such parents, obtaining from Heaven that the blessing of issue may be summarily withdrawn from them.

Curing all kinds of diseases and complaints, structural, organic, and what not? The *modus medendi* is, generally, the administering of a drop of water to the patient—hydropathy in embryo you observe; on passing the hand over the part affected—a rude form of animal magnetism. The maladies are of the class upon which the hydropathist and the mesmerist love to exercise their natural magic, such as deafness, dumbness, blindness, hysteria and nervous affections; but failures are common, and success must, I fear, be pronounced rare and unsatisfactory.

Under the third head may be ranked a vast variety of extraordinary feats, such as saving shipwrecked mariners or lost travellers, when invoked by them; appearing in person at a distance to protect a friend against unseen danger; changing females to males, seniors to juveniles, sots to scholars, sinners to saints, and infidels to Islam; saving a person's life by directing the stroke of death to another quarter; exercising dominion over birds, beasts, and fishes; causing youths' beards to grow; fasting for an unconscionable time; living without drink or sleep; watering a whole caravan with the contents of a single pipkin; ordering the wild trees of the forest to produce honey and clarified butter; restoring existence to the dead; putting to flight the Fiend and his emissaries; intuitively knowing men's minds and secret thoughts; compelling inanimate objects to act as though they had vitality and volition; breaking through walls and doors in spite of chains and fetters; visiting Hell for the purpose of saving one of its victims, and flying bodily up to Heaven.

Briefly to trace the career of a single miracle. A boat sails, we suppose, from Kurrachee to Bombay. About the Gulf of Cutch,—you recollect the Canthi of Ptolemy?—a hurricane obliges the crew to put back. During the violence of the storm, they were praying much more lustily than they were working, and being natives of the same village, they all implored the aid of one Pir,* the live patron saint of the place. Well, they were saved. In due time, when they return to their families, and talk over the affair with their friends, feeling that the adventure in its simple shape is an ordinary and uninteresting one, they begin, consciously or unconsciously, to make it more presentable by the addition of embroidery and a few ornaments. The head liar of the party,—there is one of course,—swears by the beard of the Prophet, that, as he ejaculated " Save me, Miyan Mitho!"† the form of the holy man rose before his eyes, bidding him be of good cheer, for that assuredly no harm should come to him. The rest of the crew

---

* Pir,—a saint, a man of God.

† " Reverend Mr. Sweet,"—a plebeian, but a very celebrated name in the Valley of the Indus.

either believe the invention, or wisely pretend to do
so, or foolishly lose reputation, and subject themselves to be dubbed "Atheists" by contradicting it.
The saint, on the other hand, when consulted, is sure
to declare, that, the moment he heard a sorrowful
voice calling upon his name from afar, he threw
his spirit in the direction of the sound; perhaps,
also he will condescend to accept a little present
or two.

A fair basis for carrying weight is now laid, and
the superstructure may or may not become gigantic.
If favoured by circumstance, the young miracle grows
apace in strength and station. After a few years
careful nurture and consequent development, it
changes to adult form. The ship sank to the bottom
of the sea, whence the Pir raised it with his potent
hand. Then it blooms through a glorious man-
hood of celebrity, and in green old age looks
forward to being embalmed in the leaves of some
Persian book for the instruction and edification
of posterity.

By this time you must be deadly tired of saints,
and their performances, Mr. Bull, especially as you
are one of those sturdy-minded Northerns, who do
not require everything to be

"——— oculis subjecta fidelibus,"

before it can take its seat in the penetralia of your reason and belief. Before we leave the saints, I must, however, with your permission translate that short ode which some poetic hand has inscribed upon one of the walls in honour of his Murshid, or spiritual teacher. It is, I should inform you, the production of a Sufi, a tribe of mystic devotees who hold tenets somewhat similar to the Gnostics of your faith in early days, and it teems with the commonplaces of their poetry, the negative entity of the world of matter, the positive existence of the human soul as a particle of the Eternal Spirit, enjoyment of the illusions of mundane existence, and devotion to earthly, the imperfect type of heavenly Love.

I.

They * deem the world a lovely dream,
That floats before man's wakeful eyes,
A dream of phantom weal and woe,
Unreal smiles, illusive sighs.

II.

They question not His will or why
He placed them in this passing scene,
That brings them from those blessed lands,
Thro' Memory's mist still dimly seen.

---

* The third person plural in Persian is politely used for the singular—
"they" for "he." I have retained the Oriental idiom, the present for the

III.

By them a thought, a sigh, a tear,
 In lonely meditation shed,
Are held far holier acts of prayer
 Then bended knee or bowed head.

IV.

Their Musjid's * roof is Heaven's vault,
 Its walls th' horizon's ample pale,
Its floor fair nature's vast expanse
 Of stream and sea, of hill and dale.

V.

On flowery meads, in vocal glades,
 Where tuneful choirs sing hymns of praise,
'Neath perfumed shrubs, near bubbling rills,
 They love to spend their similar days.

VI.

Their lips shrink not with Zahid's † fear,
 To taste the bright wine's bubbling kiss,
Nor shun their ears the cithern's song
 That brims their souls with happiness.

VII.

Their eyes may rest on woman's face—
 On youth and beauty's form divine,
When parted sparks of heavenly light,
 In pure and clear reflection shine.

past : the reader, if there be such a person, may consider the lines an exposition of the tenets of the sect as well as the eulogy of an individual.

* Musjid—a mosque.

† The Zahid is an ascetic to whom wine and music are abominations

VIII.

With them Love knows no carnal joys,
No sensual sweets, no low desire;
They nurse its bright and holy flame
As Guebres feed their.perfumed fire.

IX.

Their only good, good done to man;
To harm mankind, their only ill—
All other good and ill they hold
The wild caprice of mortal will.

X.

Life is to them the arch that spans
That dark abysm—Eternity;
They build not on its narrow way,
But tread it, Allah, seeking Thee.

*   *

Turning tent-wards, we come upon another venerated locality, a walled inclosure, surrounded by lofty
Peepul* trees.   During this morning's ride, I
remarked to you some places of Hindu pilgrimages, and certain upright stones stained with
vermilion and decked with huge garlands of withered
flowers upon the margin of a small deep tank, girt
round by grottos and caverns nature-cut, in the
mass of honeycombed limestone, near Kulliau Kot.
Here, again, we have traces of the same worship as

---

* The *Ficus religiosa,* a sacred tree amongst Hindoos.

that recent attempt at delineating a lady of mascu-
line habits mounted upon a peculiar breed of tiger
and lion.   The personage depicted is Singhuvani,—
the Rider of the Lion,*—a local incarnation of that
multinomial goddess, Devi, Durga, Parwati, or, as we
allegorise her, Active Virtue. If you take the trouble
to look into Moor's Pantheon, or any other popular
work upon the subject of Hinduism, you will marvel
how she earned so respectable a title in Europe,
Active Viciousness appearing to be the general
character Mythology assigns to her.†

You look towards me for some explanation of
those upright stones, daubed with red.   Mr. Bull, as

---

* The ancient Hindus knew the habits and peculiarities of the lion
well ; their modern descendants confound the name and nature of the king
of beasts with the tiger.

† Nothing can be more ridiculous than the effect produced by Hinduism,
smartly dressed up as it has been in European clothing—a system of wild
superstition, explained, emblematised, and typified by western speculators
till its very form ceases to be recognisable.

The male Triad of the Vedas, Brahma, Vishnu, and Shiva, are merely
personifications of the Almighty power, the Brahm or Demiurgos, in the
three several being-modes of Creation, Preservation, and Destruction : the
female Triad is that same power in exertion ; their very name, "Sakti"
tells us so clearly as language can.   Durga is the active destroying power
of the destroying deity, Shiva, elaborately anthropomorphised into now
an angel now a fiend—*les extrêmes se touchent*—in human shape.   To
consider her the "ideal personification of active virtue incarnate on earth,"
employing all her celestial weapons "against Maïssassoor, the buffalo-
headed demon of vice," &c., &c., is to mix a western with an eastern
idea to the utter confusion of all ideas upon the subject.

you may chance to repeat my conversation at home, I must place the seal of silence upon my lips, much as I regret so to do. But if you are not thoroughly tired of the article Faith, I can read you a lesson upon certain peculiarities observable in this corner of the world, which may set you thinking awhile.

Islam, the religion promulgated by Mohammed, was, in his day, sufficiently pure deism; the Eternal Being is as little anthropomorphised as could be expected, taking into consideration the difficulty of making the idea of one intelligible to a barbarous race. The faith conceived, born, and bred amongst the rugged hills trodden by the sons of the Wild Man, formed a *point de réunion* round which all the scattered and hostile tribes collected. For a while the human stream stood gathering bulk; presently, chafed to fury by intestine commotions, it overflowed its margin, and poured down like a desolating torrent upon the lands which lay around it.

But when the excitement of invasion and battle, massacre and plunder had passed away, the heterogeneous mass of converts forcibly incorporated with the original stock of the Faithful, found time and opportunity to shuffle a few of their old tenets and

predilections into the system of monotheism thus
forcibly thrust upon them.

The banks of the Indus were, in remote ages, the
hot-bed of Hindooism; Moultan was its strong-hold,
and Scinde was as abundant in Buddhism, as it
was in the Brahmanism that succeeded it. The
Delta had holy places in numbers, and marks of the
old religion still extend far westward of the mountains that separate us from the deserts of Mekran.
How, or at what time, the descendants of the con-
quering Arabs, made these venerated spots their own,
history, being written by themselves, of course says
not. Probably they took the first opportunity to
bury some distinguished body in any locality which
they determined to appropriate; and then, in spite
of the pagans, connected the site in question with
their own faith. One thing you may observe:—
almost every celebrated place in Scinde still displays
distinct signs of original Hindooism; moreover, the
worshippers of Brahma have Sanscrit names for this
holy incolæ of the principal mausolea, and the
Polytheist, as well as the disciple of Mohammed,
continues to attend the fairs and pilgrimages, which
periodically occur at the tombs, and other sacred
localities.

And most amusing to an indifferent observer are the zeal and violence with which the professors of the two rival creeds advance and refute their claims and right of property to the disputed person of some noted devotee.

It is related by the chronicles of antiquity, that in days gone by, and ages that have long fled, Scinde was a most lovely land situated in a delightful climate—a fertile plain traversed by the beneficent Mehran,* with large, flourishing, and populous cities; orchards producing every kind of tree and fruit, an gardens that were the reflection of Irem,† and th envy of the Seven Heavens. It was governed by powerful monarch who had mighty hosts and impreg nable forts, whose counsellors were renowned fo craft, and whose commanders were celebrated f conduct. And the boundaries of his dominions an provinces extended as far as Kanoj and Cashmere upon whose south-western frontier one of the Rahis planted two towering cypresses.

* The classical and poetical name for Father Indus, very little know beyond its banks.

† A celebrated Paradise or garden made in Arabia, by one Shedd very useful in oriental comparisons.

‡ The Hindoo Rajahs of Scinde.

During the caliphat of the Chief of True Believers, Umar the son of Khattab, it was resolved, with the permission of Allah, to subject the sinners of Scinde to the scimitar of certain sturdy saints militant. But it so happened that the captain of the Moslem armament, being opposed by a Brahman general, was killed, and, after much slaughter, his troops were discomfited, many were slain, and the rest were made prisoners.

Again, at the time when great Usman—the Lord's approval be upon him!—sat upon the seat of power, it was ordered that one Hakim, a confidential agent, should be sent to Scinde to spy out and discover the state of affairs; but the reporter caused the expedition to be abandoned by falsely * saying that the water was black, the fruit sour and poisonous, the ground stony, and the earth saline. When the caliph asked him what he thought of the inhabitants, he replied, "they are faithless."

Then during the rule of Ali—may his name be blessed!—a force passed over from Mekran, and was opposed by a large army of the hill men; but the Moslem host, calling on the Most High, began an impetuous attack, and the noise of the shouts terrified

* That Hakim must have been a most discerning traveller; his brief account of Scinde and the Scindians is a perfect specimen of pregnant truth.

the enemy, who cried for quarter whilst they fled. From that time, on occasions of conflict, the Moslem "Allahu!" is heard amongst those mountains. But when the news of the caliph's death arrived further advance was stopped.

Now the land of Serandip * is of the Ruby Islands; from this had been sent some Abyssinian slave girls, with many valuable jewels and presents for the high and mighty Emperor, Abdel Malik the Ommiade, and his deputy Hajjaj, Lieutenant of Mesopotamia. By chance the eight boats that conveyed them were driven by a storm into one of the ports of Scinde on the sea of Oman, and the robbers of the place seized them as plunder. When the agents of the King of Serandip represented that the property belonged to the caliph, they said, "if your tale be true, pay a ransom and procure release!"

In that assemblage were certain women in the purity of Islam, who had intended performing the pilgrimage to Mecca, and visiting the capital of the caliph. One of these seeing herself a captive in the hands of the uncircumcised, raised her hands to heaven and cried out thrice, with a loud voice, "Hear us, oh Hajjaj!"

This intelligence being conveyed to Hajjaj, when

---

* Ceylon.

he heard that the woman had complained thrice, using his name, he arose from his seat, unsheathed his sword, and replied, three times, "Labbayk, I attend thee!"

Umar bin Abdullah said to Hajjaj, "Commit this momentous business to me; I will proceed to El Sind and El Hind."* But, the Lieutenant replied, "I have consulted the astrologers, and they report that the period has arrived for the setting of the star of Unbelief, and for the bright dawning of true Religion in those benighted lands; in short, that El Sind and El Hind will fall to the hand of my sister's son, Mohammed bin Kasim."

In the course of days, Abdel Malik, the potent monarch, departed to his throne in paradise, and his son Walid became the Lord's Shadow upon earth in his stead. When his power was settled on a firm basis, Hajjaj urged him to renew the war with the infidels, for the purpose of releasing the Moslem captives and of punishing the Hindoo transgressors. So the new Caliph issued all necessary orders for the preparation and the equipment of a force from the public treasury.

In one month was collected an army of 15,000 men, 6000 of whom were horse, 6000 riders on

* Scinde and India.

Bukhti* camels, with 3000 foot, and five catapultas for levelling forts, together with rockets, fire-arms, and other instruments of war, as used by the unbelievers of Rum. †

The host of the Moslem marched from Mesopotamia through the province of Fars, ‡ and passed along the deserts of Mekran; then taking boat, they arrived at the mouth of the mighty Mehran, and ascended the eastern bank of the stream, to avoid the host of Kafirs § which had collected to oppose them on the western road. They advanced without opposition, till at length they saw before them, on the other side of the Indus, the tall spires and huge domes of Dewal, ‖ the principal port in Scinde.

Mohammed bin Kasim then directed the chief of his engineers to make vessels for the passage of the river, and to build a bridge, which was done by filling large canoes with stones, and by laying planks crosswise from side to side, after fastening them firmly with wedges. Then, by the help of Allah, the army of Islam began to pass over, and with showers of arrows confused the infidels that pressed forward

---

* The large dark, shaggy, two humped baggage camel, of Northern Asia.

† Constantinople.   ‡ A district in southern Persia.   § Infidels.

‖ Supposed to be the modern Tattah. It was called " Dewal," or " Debal," from its Celebrated dewalya (pagoda) ; the Arabs and Persians still know it by no other name.

to oppose them on the opposite shore. A considerable body succeeded in crossing the stream, cleared
the plain of enemies, and took up a position at the
head of the bridge until the rest of the army could
join them.

When the General had collected his host he performed the duty of Imam* at their head; and then
causing the camel saddles to be heaped up in the
form of a pulpit, he addressed the soldiery as follows:—

"The river is in your rear, the foeman in the
van; whoever is ready to yield his life, which act
will be rewarded with eternal felicity because of its
cause, let him remain and have the honour of conflict. And any amongst you, who, on further
thought, does not feel able to oppose the enemy, let
him remember that the road of flight is no longer to
be open—he will assuredly be drowned in the river,
or else fall into the hands of the Kafir. So let these
now take leave of us, for brave men determine either
to do or die."

Of the whole force, only three persons—one under
the pretence of an unprotected parent, another of a
motherless daughter, and a third of want of means—

* The "Imam" in Moslem devotional exercises is he who prays in
front of a family or congregation.

left the army. The rest declared that they were only anxious for battle.

For some days the infidels, in anxious fear and dismay, made no attempt to fight. Presently, reproached and taunted with cowardice by Jaipal, their chief, they issued in swarms from the gates, with horses sheathed in armour, and war elephants with steel howdahs; and their captain, as was the custom of the Hindoo in that day, carried during the fight an iron mace, pointed and spiked, and with it he clove the head of every warrior whom he smote. After a bloody battle, which lasted until the setting of the sun, the Moslems retired with saddened hearts; the world was yellow before their eyes; they saw nothing before them but defeat and disgrace, nought behind them but despair and destruction.

On the next morning, Jaipal again came forth with his host of armed warriors and beasts, and again he forced his way through the torrent of soldiery that opposed him. At first the army of Islam became confused; Mohammed bin Kasim, in alarm, offered up the incense of his prayers and groans at the shrine of the Most High, who favoured him, and at length vouchsafed to him the victory. Jaipal's war elephants, plied with rockets and missile fire, took flight, and in their confusion fell back upon their own people, many of whom were thus destroyed; and crowds perished at the gates of the city, vainly attempting to flee from the dagger of Destiny.

Now, in the centre of the Fort of Dewal was a place of idols, forty rods high, and on it a dome also forty rods; on the summit was a silken flag, with four tongues, the work of a potent necromantist. None of the Islamites knew this, till, on the evening of the day of victory, an old Brahman, issuing privily from the fortress, came and stood at the gate of the pavilion, in the presence of Mohammed bin Kasim.

"I learn from my books," quoth the idolator, "that this country will be conquered by the scimitar of the stranger religionist; that the appointed time is at length come, and that thou art the instrument in the hand of Fate. I am here to show thee the way.* Those before our times constructed this temple as a talisman. Until the spell is broken thy difficulty and danger endure. Order some stratagem, so that the banner on yonder dome, together with that part of the edifice, be thrown down.

Mohammed bin Kasim took thought that night. In the morning he consulted the engineer of the

---

* This reminds one of the Christian priest, who having discovered, or pretended to discover, or supposing that he had discovered, in the Book of Daniel, the future greatness of the Saracen Empire, let a party of Arabs into Damascus.

catapultas, who said, "If thou givest me ten thousand pieces of silver as a reward, I will undertake, by some means or other, to bring down the flag and cupola after three shots; if I fail, I will agree to have my hand cut off."

At the blast of the trumpet the host assembled in battle array, each cohort taking its place round the green banner that belonged to it. Every man stood silent as the dead whilst the machine, laden with a ponderous stone, was brought to bear upon its distant mark; and a universal shout of "Din! Din!"* broke from their breathless lips as the shivered flag-staff flew far away, bearing with it the talismanic banner.

Again the instrument was charged; this time its heavy load dashed against the dome, which rocked and swayed as from the effect of an earthquake. The bearded warriors then drew their scimitars, and, led by the chieftains, moved onwards in order and rank, silent with expectation.

A cry resounded from within the fort. The besieging host turned their eyes in the direction of the sound. When the veil of dust which concealed the temple floated away upon the pinions of the breeze, not a stone remained visible to mark the place where the lofty cupola once stood.

---

* "Faith! faith!" the old Arab war-cry, according to the Scindians.

Again arose the loud cry, "Din ! Din !" and the turbanded ranks, bearing the battering-rams, dashed furiously at the fortified entrance. The warders and defenders of the walls, struck with preternatural terror, fled their posts. In a few minutes the split planks and gates torn from their hinges, afforded an easy passage to the assailants. Thus was Dewal lost and won.

For three days there was a general massacre of the inhabitants. The victors then brought out the Moslem prisoners, and captured immense property and treasures.

Before throwing down the pagoda, and substituting the mosque and the minaret in its stead, Mahommed bin Kasim, ordering the attendance of the Brahmans, entered the temple and bade them show him the deity they adored. A well-formed figure of a man on horseback being pointed out to him, he drew his sabre to strike it, when one of the priests cried, " it is an idol and not a living being !" Then advancing towards the statue, the Moslem removed his mailed gauntlet, and placing it upon the hand of the image, said to the by-standers, " See, this idol hath but one glove, ask him what he hath done with the other ? "

They replied, " What should a stone know of these things ? "

Whereupon Mahommed bin Kasim, rebuking them, rejoined, " verily, yours is a curious object of worship, who knows nothing, even about himself." He then directed that the Brahmans, to distinguish them from other Hindoos, should carry in their hands a small vessel of grain, as mendicants, and should beg from door to door every morning; after which he established a governor at Dewal, and, having satisfactorily arranged affairs in that quarter, embarked his machines of war in boats, sent them up the river to Nirunkot,* and proceeded with his army by land in the same direction.

*   *   *

To-morrow morning we start early, along the beaten track, to Shaykh Radhan, the next halting ground.

* Supposed to be Hyderabad.

CHAPTER VIII.

SHAYKH RADHAN AND THE DEAD CAMEL.

WHEN we reach Jerruck, then, Mr. Bull, you have my full permission to perform a pilgrimage to the banks of the Indus, and to become as classical and intensely rapturous, or as discontented and grumblingly matter-of-fact—with you, I know, it is a toss up which —as you please. It would scarcely be convenient to visit it this dark morning, although it is only three or four miles distant; however in the appearance of the stream about Tattah there is little to interest the most excitable mind.

The shades of night seemed to be dispersed by a silvery flood which poured down upon us from the eastern sky. It scattered itself abroad in jets and streaks; then, suddenly as it appeared, the light faded before your eyes and deeper darkness than before investing the forms of earth hung from the gigantic ceiling above our heads. This is the "false dawn" as the Orientals call it. They suppose that the sun rising from his nightly couch amidst the glooms of the nether world casts his first look upon us through a hole in the mountain of Kaf,* and then rising is for a while concealed from view by the dark side and misty peaks of the fabled range.

And now appears the "true dawn," pale at first and cold, but gradually reddening and warming as the orb of day approaches the starting point of his course. It is accompanied by a damp and chilly wind, the Dam i Subh, or breath of the morning, which Moslems consider the sign that Nature is offering up her first tributes of praise and worship to the Eternal Author of her being.

You will soon be a proficient in the study of "mornings and evenings," my companion. Own that when you left England your mind was misty in the extreme upon the subject. You had a dim idea that day begins about 5 A. M., in summer, 8 in winter—your day at 9 all the year round, not with a view of dawn, but an inspection of the breakfast table. So I doubt not that all I have been showing to you is quite a novel as well as a curious sight.

This is a beautiful sunrise—generally speaking,

* A fabulous mountain, made, by Arabian geographers, to encircle the earth, and translated, in English dictionaries—why, Heaven knows—"Caucasus."

hereabouts a tame affair compared with the sunset. A bank of cloud fantastically shaped, brighter than burnished gold below where illuminated by the unrisen luminary, and darkly purpling above, lies upon a ground of glowing crimson sky, which softens off towards the upper part of heaven's dome into the sweetest imaginable rose colour. The sun

"Looks through the horizontal misty air,"

slowly topping the blurred and dotted line of the horizon that seems loth to part with his lower limb; his aspect is red and cold, as if exposed to the atmosphere of a polar latitude, and for a while he retains the egg-like form in which he first appeared to view.

This is the hour when the mighty enchantress, Refraction hight, loves to display her choicest feats. See that noble fortress, with towering keep and lofty flagstaff, rising above a long range of buildings, avenues of spreading trees radiating from it in all directions, and a broad expanse of water sleeping in its cradle of cape and promontory, and shelving shore under beetling bank and darkling hill—of what does it remind you ? Windsor Castle ?

*   *   *   ⌐

And now what do you see ? Three broken-down

hovels of wattle work, a withered tree and half-a-dozen stunted bushes on a barren plain of black mould crusted over with the glittering efflorescence of salt. No wonder that Poesy, the amiable purloiner of all nature's choicest charms, has long since made the theme her own. And no wonder that her bantlings still continue to work the subject in every possible form of common-place.

Turning from the poetical to the practical, let me direct your vision to that place full of low bastard cypress * shrubs. Do you see a pearly white drop hanging here and there from the top of a feathery branch? It is not dew, but tamarisk-honey — *turanjebin*, as the Persians call it; manna, as we have named it. A biblical acquaintance of mine discovered that this stuff was the identical article with which the fugitives from Egypt were fed in the wilderness. I ventured some objections, especially a compassion for the internals of the House of Israel—for I assure you, Mr. Bull, the effect of this turanjebin is emphatically the reverse of astringent— but quite to no purpose. He had discovered "manna in the wilderness," and preferred throwing

---

* *Alias* Tamarisk. Curious that this shrub has been confounded with the tamarind-tree by so profound an orientalist as the Baron de Sacy: " *On les eût pris pour les gros* tamarins," &c., is his mis-translation of طرفا.

out the trifling distinction between meat and medicament, to parting with his *trouvaille.**

*   *   *   *

Mr. Bull, once for all, you must not attempt to ride over bridges in the valley of the Indus. Never mind the risk of a roll down a slippery bank, or the chance of finding a quagmire in the centre of a canal, covered over with a deceitful crust of whitish hard-looking mud, or the probability of being swept off your clambering steed by a thorny branch on the far side. These are problematical, the bridge is a positive personal danger.

You are looking at that tiny raft garnished with extinguished lamps which has moored itself against the side of the broad canal which we are skirting. Yesterday was the sixth of November, in which the Diwali, a great Scindee festival, of this year came round. It is the fashion at the season to dive into futurity by means of one of the rude barques which

* My biblical friend was treading the path which greater blunderers than he had marked out. Burckhardt, following Seetzen, was also of opinion that the manna of Scripture distils from the *tarfá*, or tamarisk. These people make one lose patience altogether. The idea of feeding for forty years on a mild cathartic!

N.B.—Burckhardt is right when he states that the stuff is called " mann " (manna) by the Bedouins; but he notably deceives himself, and the truth is not in him, when, to make out a stronger case, he believes that the tamarisk now yields it, except about Mount Sinai.

you have just now remarked. The worshipper of
the river, after offering up his prayers to Father Indus
and Mother Lakshme, the Indian goddess of good
fortune, repairs in the evening to the bank of some
flowing stream, launches his craft and sits gazing at
it with an anxious eye. If dancing gaily over the
black surface, it preserves its onward career till some
bend conceals it from view, he decides that the lamp
of his life will burn brightly and steadily through
the dark course of the coming year. But, on the
contrary, should some angry surge engulf the offering
in its gloomy bosom, he prognosticates with melancholy foreboding, that his happiness or his life is
fated to meet with many a storm. In some parts of
Scinde the scene on the Diwali night is marvellously
picturesque—the black river lit up with thousands of
starlike lamps, shedding their fitful light upon sombre
bank, ruined tomb, and lofty grove.

*   *   *   *

Our road is the usual style of thing in these
regions,— a collection of trodden lines stretching over
a wide waste. We leave the silt plain upon which
Tattah stands, and ascend a hilly district formed by
the ribs of limestone rock which compose the petral
portion of this Unhappy Land's formation. Every
now and then we cross some hard, dry flat, covered

with fragments of yellowish stone; these places follow one another as steps; the highest may be a hundred and fifty feet above the level of the Indus, and the absence of tamarisk and other shrubs shows at first sight that no water, save an occasional shower of scanty rain, has been here for years.

Those tombs crowning the hill by the way side are of an unusual shape—small stone cupolas, supported by four square columns of delicate proportions. They mark the memorable spot where fell certain mighty chiefs, doing immortal deeds in some petty feudal squabble. To relate the heart of the affair would take a Scinde minstrel three good hours, and involve the recital of twenty impossibilities and about a thousand proper names, including patronymics. Intensely exciting all this would be to the Lagharis and Lasharis,* the Campbells and Chattans of this part of the world; but I fear, Mr. Bull, that it would be morphine to you. Shift the scene of Waverley to Affghanistan, or let Robert Bruce become Akhbar Khan, would it not paralyse the hand of the mightiest magician that ever created worlds with a quill?

What has halted our camels at this hour of the day?

* Two great Beloch clans.

I understand.   The lazy rascals, our servants, preferred mounting to marching, and dozing upon the soft couch of Quiet, in the shape of a load of boxes, to doing their duty in looking after our property.   The consequence was, that the brute who brought up the rear of the line, broke his nose-string, and, having no rider, shook off his burden—look at your handsome rosewood writing-desk, divided into two equal parts, connected by its Bramah instead of its hinges—and gently slipped away into the jungle, where he expected to meet a body of friends and relations.

It is no use storming at the men now; the more you scold, the less they do.   We must apply ourselves to recovering the fugitive.   Fortunately there is a village not very far off, so we shall find no difficulty in procuring the assistance of a paggi, or tracker.

The fellow rises from his slumbers under the thick cotton sheet, and stares wildly at us, as if we were the Interrogating Angels * in propriâ personâ.   We take care not to lose sight of him just at first, otherwise he is sure to play camel, and to get out of what he fancies harm's way with all possible speed,

---

* Two worthies in Moslem divinity, long since introduced by the genius of Byron to the home reader.

according to the custom of a wild country. The least the poor devil expects is the loss of his half a dozen goats, and a good beating for not being richer. That present of a rupee, however, gives him some confidence; he begins to think that we are fools; and the promise of another confirms his suspicions, and makes him courageous.

See how artistically my savage addresses him to his task. He ties on his slippers with packthread, winds his sheet tight round his waist, and squatting upon the ground, scrutinises the foot-print before he starts, with all the air of a connoisseur, making meanwhile his remarks aloud.

" He is a little, little camel—his feet are scarcely three parts grown—he treads lightly on the off fore leg, and turns this toe in—his sole is scarred—he is not laden—there he goes—*there*—*there;* he is off to the jungles of Shaykh Radhan ! Now, sain,* your slave is ready."

As we are going to pitch our tents just above that identical forest, we may send on the remaining quadrupeds with the servants, and accompany our paggi to watch his proceedings.

Is it not surprising how he runs along the trail,

---

* " Sain," in Scinde, is the " Sahib " of India, the " Sir " of England.

scarcely appearing to look at it, and yet following it
every twist and turn with the sagacity of an old
greyhound ?

We pass over beds of sheet rock, almost as
smooth as crystal; we pursue roads where your eye
and mine can see nothing but a confused mass of
fresh and faded foot-prints; we descend slopes of
hard silt, upon which you cannot detect the idea of
a mark; our tracker never stops for a moment.

Now he pauses upon the verge of the tangled
wood, but only for a brief breathing-time, and in
order to secure his shoe.

"There, Sain, I told you he was going to Shaykh
Radhan."

"Thou didst. Shahbash, be a king! (equivalent
to your "bravo!" Mr. Bull), art thou to catch him?"

"At once, Sain, he stopped here to browse, and
he has only just left the place. See, the grass has
not yet risen from where he trod."

The fellow proves the correctness of his assertion
by leading us straight up to a thicket, over the top-
most branches of which appear the fugitive's long
neck warily outstretched, and his bright black eye
nervously fixed upon us. The sight of his pursuers
seems to paralyse his energies: he feels that he
ought to wheel round and trot off without delay, but

somehow or other he cannot. The Paggi walks quietly up to him, seizes the wooden nut, still sticking in his right nostril, and tying a new string to it, secures submission without a struggle.

The Scindee is celebrated for tracking, as the Arab of Tehamah, or the Aborigines of North America. He is the only detective force the country affords, and he forms an uncommonly efficient one. If a soldier has deserted, a house has been robbed, or a traveller has been cut down, show him a footprint, and he is sure of his man. He will describe the person of the party you seek with unerring accuracy, and will follow the trail for any distance, no matter what means are taken to baffle him. Shoe your horse the wrong way, wear pads over your feet,— thieving slippers, as the natives call them,—shift from boot to nudity, and again from nudity to boot, squat, stand, spring like a kangaroo, walk on all fours like a dog, do every thing you can to throw the human bloodhound out, and still, if he be a well-trained specimen of his breed, he will catch you.

*　　　*　　　*　　　*

These camels are fated to be the death of us to-day. You see before you the encamping ground, a gravelly flat, bounded upon one side by a low, irregular line of broken and craggy hill, on the other, by a rapid descent, leading to the thickly-wooded strip of clay, which skirts the right flank of Father Indus. You could scarcely mistake the place even were I not to point it out. Look at the thousand fragments of black bottles,—in these regions, the unmistakeable tokens of the white man's presence.

You start. You clap your fingers to your nostrils. You gasp for breath upon the point of staggering. You stare around you in wonder not unmixed with horror.

There lies the cause of your plight. Some baggage camel has been left dying or dead by the travellers that last quitted this dreary spot. It is a disgusting sight: the poor beast's body in the loathsome state of transition from flesh to dust. He rests as he fell, with his long neck doubled up almost to his back, in the agonies of death; all unburied of course. A native would run the risk of twenty plagues rather than take the trouble to remove a bit of carrion. The vultures are pecking at the head and quarters with their iron bills and horrid bare necks in most uncleanly state: the crows are frantically cawing their complaints that they are not allowed to sit down to dinner by those bullies, their big brothers. And, as we approach,—I must not spare you a single detail,—two fat jackals, half torpid after their ravenous repast, creep out of their dirty dining-room in the corpse's stomach. In a few days there will be as neat a skeleton as was ever prepared by enthusiastic medical student. Even more disgusting than the sight is the scent to those who are not, like Belzoni, "fortunately destitute" of one sense. The effect of this *bouquet de chameau* upon the olfactory nerves is scarcely describable. They quiver beneath a stern smell, if I may be allowed the use of the adjective: a thing one can taste, which holds your palate and your nostrils, peoples them with its heavy effluvia, seems almost to choke you with its intensity;—many and many a year hence, Mr. Bull, when thinking of Shaykh Radhan, you will remember the sensation, and contradict the eminent phrenologist, who assures you that man cannot, by an effort of the will, recal to mind past smells.

We must not pitch here. The wind is howling madly over that platformed hill upon which the saint's domed tomb stands, but we can make the old walls a screen, and from behind these protecting heights laugh at the impotent wrath of Boreas. Our servants, I need not tell you, have lost all our iron tent pins, and as for expecting wooden pegs to hold in such a soil with such a strain upon them, it would be the height of "griffinism."

It is related of a celebrated sporting gentleman in the old country, that, on one occasion, being requested by a friend not to introduce him to the uncomfortable excitement of being overturned in a *gig or tandem, he at once ran the vehicle up against a bank and sent its contents flying into a neigbouring field.

Now, were I at all disposed to enjoy a similar, rare bit of practical wit, I have an excellent opportunity of gratifying myself. To see a single poled tent blown down in windy weather over a friend's head, is, perhaps, even more funny than pitching him out of a dog-cart. But I will content myself this time with sketching you an outline of what the spectacle would be, instead of drawing it from life.

You are sitting, we will suppose, quietly at dinner, quaffing lukewarm, muddy ale, and eating curry and dust to the sound of an aërial concert, far more powerfully than pleasantly performed.

All of a sudden, cr—a—ck!—cr'ck!! The mainstay of your canvas abode has been torn up from beneath the stone placed to keep it firm in the ground. You spring off your chair, overturning the same, and make instinctively for the exit. You are just in time to be caught and rolled over by the hinder kanat, or fly, whilst the pole, bisecting your table as neatly as the "Saladin feat" was ever performed, descends upon your humped up shoulders, and instantaneously "floors" you amidst a mass of broken boards and scattered provisions, flanked by the ruins of your washing-stand, cot, and chest of drawers, and covered over with a quantity of tent-cloth, whose weight allows you to kick, call, and struggle, but positively forbids you to escape. Up rushes your gang of domestics, jabbering and gesticulating in dire dismay,—they are owed a month's wages,—you feel a grasp, like a vice, upon your ancles, you are mercilessly drawn over the hard ground against the grain, and you display yourself once more in the face of day, with hair *à la chinoise*, white garments the colour of very brown paper, and a face, which in its mask of turmeric powder, boiled rice, dust, and the proceeds of a cut from the broken beer bottle, would scarcely be recognised by your own mother. Perhaps, the tenor of your thoughts harmonises with the exclamation of the gentleman in the "Felon Sowe :—"

> "Wist my brethren at this houre,
> That I were set in sic a stoure,
> Sure they would pray for me !"

Humph! I am not quite so certain that they would, Mr. Bull; methinks your "brethren"—

Christian and European, as well as Pagan and Asiatic—would like nothing better than to see you half brained by the roof tree which supports your somewhat too bulky abode.

Some years ago, a similar " ryghte merrie " event —for one's friends—occurred to the humble individual your guide. Substantial houses in this part of the world are built of sun-dried brick, the walls supporting rafters of Babul or Mimosa wood, over which a thick layer of mud, with perhaps a little gypsum, is spread to form a roof. The material is usually composed of saltish clay, hurriedly pounded and imperfectly mixed : you may observe that wherever it touches the ground, your abode crumbles and is scooped out by the action of humidity as effectually as if a pickaxe had been applied to the foundation. As the building, under such circumstances, is safe to fall as soon as an opportunity presents itself, the natives are careful every year to repair the weak part, and to prevent matters going too far.

Now it so happened that my corps was ordered into " country quarters " in a villainous hole called Mohammed Khan's Tanda,* on the left bank of the

* A " fortified village ;" that is to say, a bunch of houses with a wall round them.

now celebrated Fulailee River. The "village" was a square inclosure of mud wall, at least twenty feet high, for fear lest a stray breath of wind should temper the heat of the burning summer, containing some nine habitations, built much as above described, and separated by narrow lanes at least a cubit deep in dust. As the property had been let by some native chief to our Government for public purposes, the necessary yearly repairs were of course neglected.

It had been raining all night. In the morning, where dust had been, mud was, and our clay houses were literally wet through. Not dreaming of any danger, I was sitting in my "drawing-room"—an apartment comparable to nothing but a gravel-pit roofed and furnished—reading with an old Affghan Munshi his favourite Rahman's pathetic dole concerning the melancholy uncertainty and the empty vanities

"—De da dunya." *

Plump! Half a ton of wall scattered without the least warning upon the "drawing-room" floor!

Pupil and pedagogue both jumped up from their

---

* "Of this world;" part of the refrain, of a popular ode, composed by the great Affghan poet, Abd-el-Rahman, familiarly and affectionately called Rahman by his fellow-countrymen.

chairs, and in hottest haste dashed through the tatties—a kind of thorn fence, and a well-known oriental and therm-antidotal contrivance—escaped through the door in time, and only in time, to see the entrance hermetically sealed behind them; the lute used on that occasion being sundry square feet of falling front wall.

Within the twenty-four hours, three out of the nine houses that composed the Tanda lay in ruins. The things melt away after a night's rain, like ice in a London ball-room.

*   *   *   ⊤

Those three little Jheels * below us—torpid sheets of thick fluid left behind by the last inundation, with the bottom of fetid black mud baking in the sun, where the waters have been drawn off by evaporation — will afford you excellent sport. Amongst the fat sedges, tall grasses, and matted reeds, in every state of vegetable existence, from the first stage of germination to the last state of decay, you will find mallard, Brahminee ducks, bitterns, snipe, and snippets: you have only to wander into the fine acacia woods that line the banks, and a herd of half-wild buffaloes will afford you a good chance of larger stuff for the pot; and if you stay long enough with

* A lake or pond.

your feet in the water and your head in the sun, although we are getting into the heart of the cold weather, you will most probably be able to pronounce *expertus* upon the pleasures of a Scinde ague.

Fevers, I may inform you, in this part of Asia are of two kinds. One is a brisk, bold fellow, who does his work within the day, permitting you to breakfast, but placing his veto upon your dining; the other is a slow, sneaking wretch, who bungles over you for a week or a fortnight.* The former appears as a kind of small shivering, first; then as a sick headache, which, after a few minutes, feels as if a cord were being tightened round your pericranium; your brain burns as if it were on fire; your head throbs as though it would burst; your skin is hot, and hard as a riding-glove. Presently your senses leave you; to delirium succeeds congestion; you pant and puff, all your

---

* This may appear to savour of bravado, in which case the appearance is deceitful. At a distance, Yellow Jack, earthquakes, the Cuchillo, and similar strange enemies to human life, look terrible because indistinct: the heart does beat a little quicker when we fix thought upon it. But as soon as you find yourself amongst the dangers, you forget to fear them, and a little habit makes them, generally speaking, contemptible : your expected giants you find pigmies. Besides, I have been fortunate in opportunity of training, being brought up, as it were, in the midst of cholera : one easily learns to think lightly of such things in youth. And every one who thinks becomes, by some means or other, a fatalist on a small scale, after a few years in the East. " Kismet " and " Nasib " are so often, so continually, in your ears, that at last they sound themselves into a kind of reality—an entity East, a nonentity west of the Cape.

energies being applied to keeping the breath in your body—you fail therein, and are buried that evening. The slow fever attacks you much in the same way; only it imprudently allows you leisure to send for a doctor, who pours cold water from an altitude upon your shaven poll, administers mercury sufficient to stock an average-sized barometer, and blisters you, generally, with mustard and other plasters, from the nape of your neck down to the soles of your feet.

I never saw a patient recover from this necessary mode of treatment without entering into the feelings of the poor decrepit Hindu, who cursed the meddling hand which clawed the holy mud out of his mouth as he was comfortably dying upon the banks of the Ganges, and by means of a draught of " fire-water," sent him back to the world of matter, a baser bit of humanity than he was before.

   *   *   *   *

If you wish to see how peculiarly uncharming in this state of *demie-toilette* are the *appas* of a certain romantic old maid called Solitude, whom many a fool admires and courts before he has seen her, you have only to set out with me for an evening's walk. We shall not meet a human being, or descry a vestige of man's work, in the country about Shaykh Radhan.

Oh, the howling waste!

Now let us look at its denizens. High in the blue air, still catching the light of the set sun, the vulture wheels in gigantic circles, and the crows are screeching with their usual noisiness as they skelter towards their dormitory, some distant tree. The matchlock or the rifle must at some time or other have been busy upon this rugged spot, otherwise its inhabitants would not stand in such evident awe of us. See how the lynx with his tapering black tipped ears ever pricked up, slinks away, covering himself with every little bush or stone, skilfully as the best Light Bob ever drilled. The antelope stops for a moment, instinctively feeling that a foe is near, turns her graceful neck—celebrated as her eye in the Arab's poetry*—sights our advancing forms, and then, bounding off, bends her rapid course towards some region of security. That old grey boar who is slowly returning from an evening excursion to his home in the neighbouring Shikargah,† is not quite so timorous as his neighbours; he mends his pace when we approach the line of direction, but a certain look or a grunt

---

* I allude to the beautiful line of Lebid that describes the antelope bending her neck towards her newly-yeaned young.

† Hunting forest in preserve.

that accompanies the glance, gives us to understand that he has at least half a mind to revenge upon us the foul wrongs which his has sustained from the hands of our kind. We will let him pass if you please, his tusks are long, curved, and sharp as a Persian dagger, and he has a dexterity in the use of his arms which renders his practice of self-defence sufficiently imposing, especially to a walking-stick. You stand to stare at those two pugnacious animals upon the sheet of rock hard by. It is a pair of Pariah dogs, who, having had some difference upon some subject unknown, are settling the affair of honour with their natural weapons, exactly as if they were British privates fighting it out in a quiet way. A most ridiculous sight is this apparently causeless and yet most vicious and violent "set to;" they wrangle, worry, bite, roll each other over, and howl with concentrated rage as well as pain: the apparent absence of anything to quarrel about, makes the vehemence of the quarrel appear the more remarkable.

Observe in the far distance our long string of camels returning after the day's grazing in the forest. The hazy, misty atmosphere enlarges their bodies to a prodigious size: we can discern no legs, all we see is a shoal of whale-like forms floating and sinking, pitching and swaying over the successive undulations of the distant ground. Some English Eastern travellers have opined that that Great Unknown, the literato who baptised the animal, "Ship of the Desert," must have derived the idea from seeing him at a time when under the effects of the mirage his form appears and disappears on the horizon, as a vessel does upon the surface of a swelling sea. Methinks, however, the conjecture assigns somewhat too much to the power of Metaphor, and a trifle too little to the operation of Analogy.

*   ᵨ   ᴛ   ᴛ

I cannot flatter myself that I have made this day's march very interesting to you, Mr. Bull. Quite the contrary. I know it, and almost feel disposed— were I not particular upon the point of accuracy— to append a legend to that hill, or to hang a story upon this tomb. However, tomorrow may chance to bring forth an infliction of the kind.

CHAPTER IX.

THE SEVEN HEADLESS PROPHETS.

INSTEAD of marching directly upon Soondan, on the Hyderabad road, we will turn off, if you please, to the left and make for a certain fisherman's village called Kinjur.

There lies the lake, a shallow piece of water with reedy banks, and embosomed in low hills of the usual uninteresting shape, and the common unpicturesque colour. I have nothing to say about the settlement: it being the normal Scinde things, which you have seen half-a-dozen times, and I have described unto the exhaustion of synonymes. But you must allow me to slip in a few words concerning the ancient history of the place, in order to render what follows intelligible.

In the days of old—thus Asiatic legends always commence, even as European children's tales, with "once upon a time,"—here rose a celebrated city;

the capital of the Sammah* dynasty, and the seat of empire of Jam Tamachi, the son of Junur. That prince was celebrated for his beauty and valour; his open hand, like the warm showers of spring, made the hearts of his subjects expand, and his clenched fist,† like the icy breath of the Destroyer, paled the cheeks of his rivals and his foes. He was truly the shadow of the Lord cast upon earth's face: he sat upon the cushion of sovereignty firm as the tall hill that spreads out its giant skirts upon the subject plain: both the storms of foreign war and the shocks of internal disturbance were equally unavailing to shake the basis of his prosperity.

Before proceeding any further, you, Mr. John Bull, are humbly requested not to confound my prince's title with any description of conserve—raspberry, strawberry, or other.‡ "Jam," meaning a chief or the head of a clan, is the titulary appellation of the Sammah rulers of Scinde.

In the fifth year of the magnificent Jam Tamachi's

---

* A Scindee tribe that ruled the country for many years before it fell into the hands of the Mogul.

† In Persian metaphorology, the open hand is the symbol of generosity; the closed fist, of austerity, avarice, or violence.

‡ This deprecation is not unnecessary. Mr. Fraser altered his " Kuzzilbash," to the " Persian Adventurer," because John Bull, with " Callipash," I suppose, or " guzzle and hash," ringing in the honest fellow's ears, pertinaciously believed it to be an *oriental cookery-book.*

reign, Bahaeldin,* the majestic saint of Multan, being urgently invited, by his disciples at Tattah, to grace the fair land of Scinde with his presence, was induced to comply with their requests. To such an extent did he delight men's minds by his spirit-stirring words and deeds, that the said disciples—may their and their father's graves be desert!—abominably resolved to kill him and eat him;† expecting thereby to secure to themselves the perpetual benefit of his presence, and to raise their recreant selves to a high degree in the spiritual world. However, they were defeated in the design. One of the saint's trusty followers discovered the plot, proposed to save his superior by sleeping in his bed that night, and was graciously permitted to enroll himself in the ranks of that distinguished body of men—the Moslem army of martyrs. The accursed Murids ‡ then took

* Popularly called Bahawalhakk—signifying it matters very little what. His name is invoked by all the Moslem tribes, from Multan southwards, and his very curious biography has been made the subject of many and many a tedious volume.

† A strange way, you remark, to propitiate a holy man—a very common one, I assert, in the wilder parts of Central Asia, as any sceptic may learn by asking the Affghan Hazarehs, how they came by the number of Saints buried on their mountains. As regards eating the venerated defunct, it is done with the superstitious, popular idea that whoever tastes the flesh or blood of a great Santon, thereby eats himself holy, as the Templars dine themselves "learned."

‡ A Murid is a "disciple," opposed to a Murshid or "spiritual instructor."

the corps, "bryttled" it, boiled the choice cuts, and were preparing for their cannibal repast, when— O never failing expedient in the hands of the Eastern romancer!—struck with an unknown fear they looked loathingly upon—

"The poor remains of what was once a saint;"

put them into a pot and cast it upon the bosom of Mehran. The vessel was presently found by seven hungry men of the fisherman caste, who devoured its contents in ignorance of their nature, and at once by virtue of the same, quitting vulgar piscation became fishers of humanity, and men of God, very holy, and, apparently, very fond of meddling with matters that did not quite concern them.

You see that tall, old ruin of hewn stone upon the hill overlooking the lake. It was built there by Jam Tamachi, for the purpose of affording his beautiful bride Nuren, the daughter of a fisherman, a view of the humble scenes in which she was born, and which, incredible to relate, she continued to love even after her elevation to the dizzy height of regal dignity. To that palace the seven Walis* repaired, and demanded the right of ingress in so authoritative

* Wali, a saint.

a tone and manner that the very warder, an order of
" gentlemen" who, in Scinde, are not more affable
than the footmen of Belgravia, dared not turn up
their noses at the sight of pedestrians knocking at
a great man's door. And when these individuals
appeared in the presence, instead of joining their
palms, prostrating themselves, trembling and looking
exanimate with fear, Pom ! they squatted down upon
the rich rugs, and stared in the prince's face for at
least five minutes. Cats, be it observed, are by
proverb allowed this privilege in England; but, Mr.
Bull, in a purely oriental country, a low fellow ven-
turing to try the experiment, would probably leave
the hall of audience plus a solid bastinado and minus
half the number of toes that usually terminate the
human frame. No wonder, then, that the Jam,
just and generous as he was, could not for the life of
him prevent his cheek turning livid and his beard
becoming crisp with rage.

" King of kings ! we are here by order of
Heaven to protect thee and thine against the
impious attempts of the Mogul ! "

The Jam's beard re-became limp.

Unacquainted with Scinde history, you must be
informed that the high and mighty Aladdin, Emperor
of Delhi, had fixed the eye of concupiscence upon

the fair form of Scinde, and, like certain modern rulers, by no means contented with the Indus—the "natural boundary of Western India"—as a frontier, he had been doing all his possible to fix a quarrel upon the Sammah chief; and the latter, knowing that the weakest always goes to the wall in Asia as in Europe, had smilingly put up with many an insult and injury. Hence the reason why, when the Mogul was alluded to, the Jam's hairs returned to their normal state, whilst an expression of curiosity and encouragement replaced the gloom which had settled upon his countenance.

The seven fishermen then proceeded to inform him, that directly under the walls of the capital was the head of a large land serpent, whose tail terminated at Delhi—two thousand miles or so, allowing for an occasional coil. They added, that as long as the animal in question continued in that position, Scinde had nought to fear from the Lords of India, and concluded by asking and obtaining the Prince's permission to thrust an iron spit into the unoffending reptile's nose, for the purpose of curbing any erratic propensities which it might be disposed to indulge in.

Long and loud laughed the people of Tattah at the senile credulity of the Jam, their ruler. They had no "Charivari," it is true, but the want of that civilised invention was more than compensated by the infinitude of sarcastic odes and sneering epigrams that issued daily from the local pens. Now Tamachi, like many other great people, ancient and modern, had a nervous horror of the hum, the buzz, and the sting of that spiteful little insect, called a satirist. Moreover, although he knew that his only chance of escaping with a whole skin was to remain dead quiet till the swarm that had settled upon him thought proper to seek another subject, he could not bring his impatient spirit to act so sensibly. The result of his irritability was, that after vainly threatening to impale, roast, or chop in pieces the authors of the nuisance, and after enduring its increasing virulence for a few days, at length, in an evil hour, he ordered that the spit should be wrenched out of the ground.

The iron was pulled up reeking with gore, and was shown to the sceptical Tattaites. Then the sneer of scorn and the smirk of self-esteem gave way to quite another kind of look. They fell upon their knees before the Prince and his holy advisers; awe-struck and confounded into belief, they supplicated the seven fishermen to intercede with Heaven for them, their children, and their country. But these personages informed them that the thing was impossible, that the snake had

" Turned his head where stood his tail,"

and that Scinde had for ever lost her protecting spell.

Jam Tamachi, as I have said, was renowned for exceeding equity.   He acknowledged that the fishermen were in no wise blameable: indeed he owned that their conduct throughout the affair had been everything it ought to have been.   Only he insisted upon the paramount importance of obedience in the subject, and told them flatly that unless that serpent's head returned to where it was before, within the twenty-four hours, he should consider it his melancholy duty to make their pates and the rest of their persons part company.   Justice, he remarked, was a very fine thing, but—

His arguments are not worth recording.   The fact is he was unconsciously conscience-smitten; angry with himself, a person which he could not punish, he naturally became anxious to find some one upon whom he could vent his royal rage.   The seven fishermen asked for nothing better than the crown of glory.   So Jam Tamachi obliged them in that little matter by directing their throats to be cut from ear to ear, and their heads to be rudely wrenched off their bodies. Which was done with all the honours.

But conceive the dismay of the king, his courtiers, his counsellors, his captains, and his subjects, when the last corpse immediately after decapitation, rising slowly from the cordovan carpet, upon which it knelt during the operation, stood bolt upright, grasping its head in its outstretched right hand. And furthermore, imagine if you can, the state of mind in which the terrified throng heard the blood-less lips pronounce this unpoetic rhyme—

> " Dyke of Aror be burst, and flow
>   Hakro perennial to the main :
> Swim ye fish, ye lilies grow
>   Where Sammahs plough the sultry plain !"

Now the bund or embankment of Aror * had, hundreds of years before the time of Jam Tamachi, been thrown across the Indus by the masonic prowess of an honourable husband, who to save his fair spouse from the tyrant Dilu Rahi's † importunities, diverted the main stream into its present rocky bed, and escaped from the ruthless king's capital, *viâ* the new cut. As for Hakro flowing, no one thought it

* Aror, a city once celebrated in Scinde, is located by antiquaries about four miles eastward of the Indus at Sukkur and Rohri.

† See Chap. v.

possible that the old dried-up bed would ever be restored to its pristine state; and yet there stood a corpse pertinaciously and positively assuring them that the Sammah tribe of Scindees, who for the most part inhabit the sandy and sterile eastern frontier towards Jesulmere, should dine on such luxuries as pullah * fish and aquatic roots.

Satisfied apparently with the amount of commotion caused by its display of eloquence, the corpse turned upon its heel and deliberately walked out of the audience hall, through the crowded streets in the direction of the Desert.

Then arose the second sufferer, and with the malicious eagerness with which man communicates bad news to man, pronounced these prophetic words—

"Steeds, gaunt and blue,† pour from the North,
    And matrons walk the crowded way:
Then, Scinde ! incline thy stubborn head
    Unto the strangers'‡ sabre sway."

That individual left the palace amidst a fresh thrill

---

*, The "sable fish," hereabouts a favourite article of food. See Chap. xxviii.

† A grey horse, in Persian and Scindee, is called "blue." The people could not but think of this prediction when they saw our cavalry, who are generally mounted on light-coloured Arabs, marching down from Sukkur to attack Hyderabad.

‡ In the original "Tajyani," a word with a plurality of signification, or, rather, none at all in particular.

of horror.   Besides the sceptre of Delhi, the natives
of Scinde only feared the Affghan sword.   Affghanistan, you know, Mr. Bull, is north of Scinde, and
the idea of their already too gay dames and too
coquettish damsels being allowed to go about the
streets and bazaars without any let or hindrance
whatever, was too hard for them to stomach.   The
threat of slavery, the "tail of the storm," fell almost
unheeded upon their ears, so stunned were they by
the outburst that preceded it.

The third corpse, probably in pity of their mental
tortures, changed the subject and became extremely
oracular and ambiguous—

"For years to come broad Ar shall flow;
But when it dries by Fate's decree,
The fierce Beloch shall sell his son
For silver pieces two and three."

Now the Ar or Bhagar, the western outlet of the
Indus, was of no particular importance to the
people of Tattah: moreover, in those days, they
knew little and cared less about their future rulers,
the Belochies, a tribe of hill barbarians.   Modern
Scindians would have recognised in a moment the
mystic meaning of the quatrain, which points
unerringly to the social position of that people in
the present day, when the descendant of a Talpur or

royal Beloch and the progeny of a Machhi* are equal
as two pennyweights in the well-poised balance which
British Equity holds before an admiring world.

But lest the crowd should, we must suppose,
think themselves quite out of the scrape, corpse
number four, after going through the usual pre-
liminaries, began to predict a direct and direful
disaster :—

> " I hear from Lar the sound of strife,
>   I see the hosts from Siro haste ;
> Then, Scinde ! from 'twixt the South and East
>   The brand of war thy shores shall waste."

Here was a terrible conglomeration of misfortunes;
a war beginning from Lar (Lower Scinde) ; again
the prospect of those abominable Affghans attacking
Siro (the upper districts), and the certainty that both
provinces would be involved in the common calamity.
Intensely bitter became the reflections of the
Tattaites when the current of their thoughts was
diverted by another prediction, which acted upon
the mental palate like a sugar-plum after a black
dose—to reverse Tasso's most epic image.

> " Karo Kabaro's walls shall view
>   Fierce combat raging half a day ;
> The Mirmichi shall routed be,
>   Then, Scinde ! once more be blithe and gay."

---

* A low caste of Scindians.

And the doubt as to who or what these Mirmichi*
might be, by exciting the curiosity, aroused the
spirits of the auditors in no ordinary degree. They
actually experienced a sort of pleasurable excitement
—as Italians do when miracles are performed—as
the next headless body, rising from its knees, followed
the example of its vaticinating brotherhood :—

> " The Mirmichi ! who may teach ye
>   The surest token him to know ?
> His lady fair wears double tails,
>   And down his neck the long curls flow."

The King and all the crowd, who knew for certain
that their own hair was regularly every morning, after
being washed with clay,† and perfumed oil, combed
out and tied in a knot upon the poles of their heads,
and that the locks of their beloved spouses were
plaited into a single *queue* with scarlet ribbons and
strings of seed pearl, now felt assured that the
rough handling predicted for the Mirmichi—common
fellows who did not know even how to make their
heads look decent—could not by all the quibbling
and quirking, the twisting and torturing of any
authority upon the subject of mantology in the land,
be made to apply to themselves. Had they been an
English audience they would most probably have

---

* The word has no precise meaning.   † See Chap. II.

greeted the speaker with a loud hear, hear! or a general cheer. Being Scindians they gesticulated and jabbered till the last defunct — determined that as his brethren had begun to "curry favour" with the ignorant of caviare he would not be out-done 'in pandering to popularity,—rapped out these words :—

> "Come, come, ye men ! and sit in peace
> Beneath the Nagar's* sheltering shade :
> Beyond Puran no roof-tree plant,
> Nor let one hearthstone there be laid:"

and, following in the steps of his fraternity, left the Durban.

When the predicting was all over, crowds, as you may imagine, followed the predicters in order to see what became of them. They must have had the vitality of worms, and the legs of horses, those holy men, for they walked right on end with a most important bit of themselves under their arms, to the banks of the Puran River, at least a hundred miles off. At length reaching a place called Amri, they fell to the ground bereft of motion, and were there buried by those who had the curiosity to watch this peculiar display of pedestrianism to the last.

* The name of *Tattak*, Chap. VI.

Their sepulchres, which are shown to the present day, prove, or ought to prove, I suppose, that what is said to have occurred, occurred.

Some of these rugged rhymes are palpably of modern growth; others are ancient, and have probably been handed down from father to son for generations past.* You would scarcely believe, Mr. Bull—unless at least you heard it from so well-informed a *compagnon de voyage* as myself—the effect they have exercised upon the fortunes of this province. The Lycophronic designation " Mirmichi," after being applied successively to the Indians, Affghans, Jats, and others, descended in due course of time to the next ruling race, the Belochies. *Variæ lectiones* began to creep in. The last couplet of the sixth corpse's *quatrain* was thus amended :

" Their locks are black as jet above,
    Their raiment darkly blue below :"—

a description applicable to the inhabitants of half

* Who will write us a work on uninspired prophecy ? It ought to be a most amusing and a most interesting one. The eastern world is full of curious predictions ; for instance—

The Chinese expected harm from a foreign tribe ruled by a woman.

The Burmese learned from their Merlin that they should be invincible, until a ship, without oars or sails, stemmed the rapid course of the Irawaddy.

And, to quote no others, the wild tribes of Southern Africa, as the accomplished authoress of the " Cape and the Caffres " informs us, felt prepared to be beaten when they saw the long-foreseen sea-waggons touch their shores.

Central Asia. When, after many petty squabbles with Bombay—so they interpreted the origin of the storm from between south and east—a force marching from Lower Scinde, under Sir John Keane, threatened them with war; and finally, when Sir Charles Napier, hurrying down from Sukkur with his cavalry, mounted on gaunt "blue" steeds, the self-named "Mirmichi" felt certain that their hour was come. They fought, but with diminished spirit, like the garrison of Bhurtpore when besieged by their fated capturer the "Lord Alligator." * Thus the prediction, as we so often see in such matters, verified itself. To the present day the Scindians swear by these prophecies; the Bhagar creek is gradually shrinking, the proud Beloch has lost all the privileges which he once enjoyed as the ruling race; ladies do walk the streets much more than they used to do, and Kurrachee, "beneath the Nagar's shade," (i. e. not far from it) has ousted Hyderabad, from its ancient position, as capital of the country. True the dyke of Aror remains, the Hakro has not yet provided the hungry Sammahs

* It was predicted that Bhurtpore was impregnable to anything but a Kumbheer or alligator. "Kumbheer meer" would mean the "Lord Alligator," and sufficiently resembled Combermere to sound uncomfortable in Hindoo ears.

with any fishes, and there has been no battle at the place called Karo Kabaro.   But these are little flaws which must be regarded with the indulgence usually extended by you, Mr. Bull, to poesy, painting, and the other trades which deal wholesale in imaginative material.

Pray look not so contemptuous and high-minded at what you term the "poor devils' superstition and credulity."   These are weeds which grow all the world over, in every age and in every clime.   Whenever the public mind, civilised or barbarous, becomes excited, it flies directly to the marvellous, the preternatural, and the supernatural, even as a gentleman in distress does to the bottle.

I could elucidate this assertion by many an example, but not having time to dress and deck it in the elaborate garb it deserves to wear, I prefer, with your permission, to leave it in the naked form of a *dictum*.   But before parting with the subject, I recollect reading a legend in some old French book—name long since forgotten—which matches so admirably with what I have just been narrating, that for the life of me I cannot help narrating it in my own way for your edification.

As one Dennis, of beatified memory, was trudging in company with a little knot of friends towards a muddy town and camp, called Lutetia Parisiorum, then garrisoned by a legion of pagan Romans, he came upon one of their outposts on a hill not far from the end of his journey. The spirit moved the holy Areopagite to turn into one of the leathern tents, tenanted by the fighting men, and to begin a discourse which presently collected around him half a century of soldiers, and hundreds of the Lixæ, or camp followers.

The harangue—I take the liberty of presuming, for such is almost invariably the case—began with an exhortation to the men-at-arms, about mending their ways, figuratively, not literally, and becoming Christians. From which proper field for good advice and much prosing, it slipped insensibly into a debateable dangerous bit of ground, violent abuse of heathenism, and all heathens, young and old, male and female, priests, laymen and vestal virgins, pell mell.

" *Id nimis est bonæ rei,*"—that's too much of a good thing,—said a frowning old Triareus, or grenadier, six feet and a half high, with a beard like a bear's back, and a face gridironed with scars.

" *Fac teneat maxillam tunc,*"—make the parson cove hold his jaw then,—cried a pert Veles, or light infantry man.

" Nothing easier—*hic it*—here goes," growled the

veteran ruffian, walking off to the tent of his centurion.

The *vieille moustache* was right. Captain Caius Flaccus Luscinus Æmilianus Indicus—he derived his second cognomen, or agnomen, from having served twenty years in India with the * * Buffs—disliked nothing more than a Frenchman, save and except only a Christian. Military law was not quite so deeply studied, or so well defined in those days as it is now. So the gallant officer found little difficulty in making out a case of felony against the holy St. Dennis and his friends, who, by the by, had done absolutely nothing but shake over their bare feet at the prospect of appropinquate martyrdom. All were seized at once, were unmercifully kicked and mauled, lest decapitation might not be a sufficient punishment, and finally were beheaded with extreme brutality, for their clothes formed so ragged a perquisite, and their pockets were so painfully light, that no amount of supplication would induce Calcraftus, the lictor, to do his work like a gentleman.

The saint was the last to suffer. In the fervour of his orisons, he had quite-forgotten one thing, namely, that his bones, which might be so useful in healing the bodies and souls of mankind, would be quite lost to the world, if thrown, as they were likely to be, into the nearest ditch, to moulder away in obscure corruption. So, leaving his six friends, whose faith did not enable them to perform such achievements, St. Dennis rose from the blood-stained ground, and carrying his head—whose frontal portion frowned like a Saracen's upon the discom-fited pagans—in his hand, he walked directly into the "City of Mud," where, after a short consultation with the Very Reverend the Diocesan of that diocese, he was duly "put to bed with the shovel," in the firm and pious hope of becoming, at some future time, a ton of reliques.

I forget whether the hard heart of Captain Caius Flaccus Luscinus Æmilianus Indicus was melted by the occurrence, or whether he died, as he lived, a pestilent heathen. But I perfectly recollect, that there is, near Paris, a place called Montmartre, the Mount of Martyrs, and, I consider the name proof positive that the event above detailed really occurred.

And, Mr. Bull, you cannot need reminding, that during the last few years —48, —49, —50, and —51, all kinds of Welsh and German predictions about crowned heads, war, famine, and grave-diggers have been flying about in the mouths of men. None, of course, believed in, though all knew and quoted them: but had they turned out true, which unfortunately they did not, they had at least as fair a chance of descending to posterity as the rhymes of the Seven Fishermen.

CHAPTER X.

SOONDAN AND JERRUCK.

Two places to which I am about to introduce you, rather for the ceremonial and uniformity of the thing than with the expectation that you will derive much pleasure from the acquaintance.

I dare say, the journey from Kinjur to Soondan, the nearest village in the Hyderabad road, was thus noted in your diary:

"Rose early, mounted old Arab, lost the way three times; cold and comfortless; did not arrive at encampment-ground till nine; five hours doing ten miles! Place where tent stood, dirty and disagreeable. Breakfasted as usual, slept, awoke at 2 P.M. Splendid afternoon. Dined at three; at four, walked a mile or two to see some large domed tombs; I am sick of them, but that fellow B. will insist upon my visiting all the sights. All to be seen was a troop of beggars, calling themselves 'Fukyers,' who looked very surly before I gave

them a few coppers. Returned to tea; went to
bed under quilt first time since leaving dear old
England."

And I have no doubt, oh you unromantic old
fellow! that you chronicled the next day's march in
a very similar style.

We started, you may remember, *en route* for
Jerruck, winding along the skirts of many ridgy
heights, now descending into the thickly-wooded
plain that lines the margin of the river; then again
ascending the stony hills that constitute its western
barrier.

About half way we passed through a long Shikargah, which has gained a perdurable ill name. This
is supposed to be the hunting forest where those
flinty-hearted despots, the Talpur Amirs, " like the
first Norman in Bolderwood, razed a populous village
to the ground, and exiled its inhabitants to a distant
district, because the crowing of the cocks and other
rural sounds of its human and bestial population dis-
turbed the game in the neighbouring preserve."

When you are in the highly moral and philan-
thropic mood,—you are liable to such complaints
by fits and starts, Mr. Bull,—what food for reflection
and dissertation does such a fact afford you! The
stony bosom of despotism,—Nero and his harp,—

William the Conqueror and William surnamed Rufus,—" the *caput mortuum* of tyranny distilled down step by step, from its first outbreaks in the insolence of place and the intoxication of success, till it ends in the destruction of *villages* (the plural), and the expulsion of a *population* (rather an extensive singular!) for the ·creation of hunting ground." These, I repeat, are pregnant themes.

Then came to mind that dear old Oliver's rod-taught lines upon the subject of deserted villages, teeming with images of lovely ruralities and romantic ideas of purity and happiness, which your boyish fancy was most erroneously wont to associate with country life. With what fervour you recited that beautiful passage:—

> " As some tall cliff that lifts its awful form,
> Swells from the vale, and midway leaves the storm,
> Though round its breast the rolling clouds are spread,
> Eternal sunshine settles on its head."

Not that the quotation was very *à-propos*,—but still. And though grim Reason suggested, that these Caligulas of Scinde had a perfect right to do what they pleased with their own property, how willingly you turned an ear to the small, still voice which informed you that the ruin of that ungodly race was the retributive decree of Providence.

However, about all this there is a great deal of misapprehension, the growth, I conceive, of a hotbed of "humbug." It is a curious illustration of Sathanas and his scriptural quotations, that whenever good Madam Britannia is about to break the eighth commandment, she simultaneously displays a lot of piety, much rhapsodising about the bright dawn of Christianity, the finger of Providence, the spread of civilisation, and the infinite benefit conferred upon barbarians by her permitting them to become her subjects, and pay their rents to her. Examine this omni-quoted Shikargah tyranny-grievance. In Scinde each component house of a flourishing village would be razed to the ground, carried bodily ten miles off, re-erected and re-inhabited at the probable expense of two shillings and sixpence per domicile. Moreover, I regret to say, that the Scindians, like foreigners in general, having no word to explain your "home," attach none of those pretty ideas to the place in question, which supply Mr. John Bull, Mrs. B. and the children, with matter for eternal maudlin.

You remarked, as we passed through, the dry grass smouldering under our horses' hoofs. This Shikargah appears to have a "fatal facility" of catching fire: I have passed through it half a dozen times, and always found some part of it burning. Here it was that three fine young officers of the 2nd Queen's, then marching northward under Sir John Keane, lost their lives. A court of inquest assembled, and recorded a verdict of accidental death. The men of the regiment, of course, were furious, as they had a prospect of fighting the Belochies; and, although there was no evidence to prove that the enemy had been guilty of foul play, like soldiers generally at such a conjuncture, they were more than willing to find something to be immensely ferocious and blood-thirsty about. This is the way in this part of the world. You seldom hear of men going into battle without some aggravated personal grievance, such as the loss of an officer, a friend, a dog, a wife, or a box. One old Scotchman, in Affghanistan, never spared a life, it is said, because the women were in the habit of crying out "amán!" (quarter!) which Sawney, translating into a petition for "a mon," considered a liberty so gross as to justify any amount of severity.

Probably the poor fellows had set fire to the jungle in order to start the game, and a sudden change of wind had brought the flame down upon them. You can scarcely imagine how easy it is to be burned to death in one of these places. All beneath the tall tamarisk, acacia, mimosa, and poplar trees,* is a mass of matted underwood, luxuriant sedge, rank weeds, and long grass, which in the dry season are inflammable as German tinder. Your servants and camels pass through the first, say an hour before you, smoking their pipes and dropping the fire in all directions. You follow them probably by another and neighbouring cut, jogging slowly along, thinking of breakfast or whistling for want of other occupation. Suddenly a sharp crackling and a loud roaring behind you make you prick up your ears; you look round and see a huge tongue of flame playfully attempting to lick your back. In a frantic state of mind you clap spurs to your steed, and if fear do not deprive him of the use of his limbs, or if on the other hand, fear do not urge him onward so blindly that the bough of a tree sweeps you off his back; if the path before you be not bright with red-hot ashes upon which no horse will tread; and finally, if the fire fail to catch you up behind, or to meet you in front—for one of these five contingencies you must be prepared—escape is possible. *Vice versâ*, there will be a Court of Inquest. If on foot you are sure to ascend some tree, an act

---

* The bhan, a kind of poplar, is the most remarkable tree in this part of Scinde.

of infatuation which no one, situated as you are, fails to commit; you are asphixiated by dense rolling clouds of hot black smoke spangled with little bits of burning straw; the flames are roaring for you below; you leap wildly from your ill-selected place of refuge; you speedily become a " distressing spectacle."—

*   *   *   *

As, mounting the brow of a hill, we caught sight of a line of water inclosed by jungly banks still purpling in the imperfect morning light, I elevated myself, if you recollect, upon my stirrups, extended my right arm, and with the impressive expression of countenance with which an effective cicerone standing at the Camaldoli, pronounces the apophthegm, "Vedi Napoli e poi muori," I looked at you and exclaimed—

"There, Mr. Bull, lies the far-famed, the classic Indus ! "

Now, a year or two after your return home you will probably forget *les actualités* of the scene. You will find it necessary to suppose facts, as you will have discovered that the Childe Harold style "goes down," society's throat much more glibly than that of Matthews or Smollett—the querulous and the *blasé*—therefore you will become impressionable, romantic, poetical, semi-sublime, *et cetera*.

And one of these days, sir, when I detect you describing to a delighted lady audience "the strong —the overpowering emotion with which you contemplated the scene of Alexander's glories:" when I hear you solemnly asseverating that "never before did the worship of water or water-gods appear to you so excusable, as in observing the blessings everywhere diffused by this mighty and beneficent stream,"—

Then, sir, I shall whisper in your ear, "No, Mr. Bull, you did nothing of the kind. You looked surlily at me when I attempted to kindle the fuel of enthusiasm latent in your bosom, and you remarked that the river wasn't broader than the Thames at Black'all. This you corrected to the Thames at Green'ich, and between Greenwich and Blackwall you stuck till we reached the margin of the stream. Then you swore that it was still as a mill-pond, foul as a London sewer, shallow, flat-banked, full of sand islets,—briefly, an ugly sight. Even the lovely acacias, whose yellow locks drooped gracefully over the wave, as if they were so many Undines gazing fondly into their natal depths, could not force a single expression of admiration from you."

*   *   *   *

Jerruck is the first town you have seen not built

upon the alluvial flat formed by the Indus. It occupies the summit of an irregular height, the last of the broken chain over and along which we have travelled. These hills generally rise about one hundred feet above the plain, and have flat tops with areas of different extents varying from fifty yards square to half a mile or so. The span of rock upon which the town is built, forms a headland projecting into the river, and thus checks its excursions towards the westward.

The cantonment is slightly fortified. You see below the town that hard dry plain composed of sandstone and covered with a *débris* of iron ore instead of the vegetable matter one usually expects plains to produce. At one time that was considered a good position for a large garrison, as it commands the navigation of the river, would never want good water and supplies, and is situated in a healthy climate near a place of some importance—the grand mart to which the wild mountaineers of Belochistan resort for pleasure and profit. At present Jerruck is only an outpost, the garrison consisting *in toto* of a company of sepoys detached from a regiment at Hyderabad, with a solitary lieutenant to command and drill them. Some time ago here, was the head-quarter station of the Camel Baggage Corps, a mixture of men and beasts, very efficient in time of war, but uncommonly expensive in peace, compounded by the conqueror of Scinde as a sedative to another complaint in the constitution of the Indian army, namely, the inconceivable quantity of kit and baggage with which we are popularly supposed to be in the habit of marching. What terrible things these pet grievances are!

*   *   *   *

We have not spent an exciting day. The " officer commanding at Jerruck," after receiving our official reports of arrival, paid us a long visit, but, as often happens, the poor fellow has become quite an Orson, and has utterly forgotten that there are any topics of conversation but shikar—sport and his paltan or battalion. We passed an hour or two pleasantly enough in directing our spy-glasses at the ladies, who were disporting themselves in the muddy waters of the " Classic." After which, we walked through the town, were barked at by the pariah dogs, stared at and called Kaffirs by the little children—blessed effects of British liberty! giggled at by certain fair dames with roguish eyes, and avoided by the rest of the population. But we did not remain long in the streets: I know no place where one of your thorough-bred continental-English

flaneurs would be more out of place than in a Young
Egypt town. Descending the western side of the
hill, you remarked an attempt at sculpture, a huge
misshaped form which I informed you was Hanuman,
the Hindoo monkey-god. And I took the opportunity to remark that the worshippers had just
decorated his countenance with a coat of vermilion,
not solely for the purpose of rouge, but as a compliment to his baboon deityship—a practice anciently
western as well as eastern. Then we stood for a
few minutes to see a native horseman, one of the
mounted police, which acts the compound *rôle* of
gendarmerie and Cossacks in these regions, exercising his charger on the plain below; teaching him to
bound off at full speed when he felt the heel; to stop
dead, with the best chance of injuring his back sinews,
when the rein was drawn; to canter over a figure
of 8, gradually contracting its dimensions till the
quadruped leant over at an angle of 45°, and to gallop
like mad whilst the owner threw himself over the
off-side, and hanging by his left heel to the cantle,
picked up his spear from off the ground. Then we
returned home to dinner, and now here we are—
sitting upon the banks of the Indus, and wondering
what we are to do next.

I recollect a somewhat curious event which occurred at Jerruck, and as it illustrates certain oriental states of mind and phases of feeling which you, Mr. Bull, have long since forgotten, I will forthwith recount it to you.   Before Scinde was thoroughly settled by our bayonets, little Jerruck was committed to the safety of one Agha Khan, a Persian noble, who, having fled his native country in consequence of an attempt at rebellion ridiculous even in that land of eternal ridiculous rebellions, turned *condottiere*, and with his troop of ruffians took service under us. Receiving orders to garrison the town, the worthy descendant of the ancient Ismailiyah chiefs * at once assumed command, issued proclamations directing the timid inhabitants to board and lodge his men gratis, levied a kind of tribute from all who could pay it, unmercifully bullied all who could not, and, in short, invested himself with all the outward and visible signs of royal rank and dignity.

Some weeks the Agha spent in his new kingdom, leading a life after Sancho Panza's own heart; perhaps exceeding a little in the drinking and love-making lines.   His followers following his example, " eat, swilled, and played," till Jerruck became

---

* A sect that had the power of producing the Old Man of the Mountain, of whom Christendom has heard and read so much.

another Nineveh on a very small scale. The Belochies, having nothing better to do, had threatened to attack it a dozen times or so, but the Agha laughed at their beards. Were they not hogs of Sunnis ? * Had he not dishonoured all their mothers ? And had he not done the strangest possible things to their father's graves? Whose dogs were they that they should dare to face the death-dealing scimitar of the Iroonee ? †—mouth the word well.

A parenthesis! Collect the noted liars and boasters, the Munchausens and Gascons of both hemispheres, I will back the first pure Persian I chance to pick up against the whole field.

One evening the Agha had just finished his dinner, and was preparing for a game of back-gammon or chess, which he was sure to win, as no man dared to win it from him; the drinking-cups and the bottles were ranged in a line before him; the musicians were twanging and howling in a corner of the room; every thing was prepared for a quiet " at home ; "—

When all of a sudden, half-mad with fear, rushed

---

* The Agha was a Shieh—a Protestant, as it were,—*versus* a Sunni, or Romanist.

† Iran, generally pronounced Iroon, Persia ; Iroonee, a Persian.

in an unfortunate Scindee, bringing the intelligence
that a body of at least fifty thousand Belochies—
two of the cyphers were as usual *de trop*—had
arrived within a mile of Jerruck, that he himself
had seen them, and had hurried on to give the Agha
warning, lest he and his heroes should be attacked
unawares.

You, Mr. Bull, or I, under such circumstances,
would most probably have given the fellow a handful
of rupees, and then would have turned out to inspect
the guards, and to make preparations for a set-to—
possibly dispositions for a retreat, should such
measure be deemed advisable.

"Seize that pup of unmarried parents," roared
the Agha in tremendous wrath; "here with the
pole! Where are the rods, ye dog-papas?"*

The attendants, thus designated, indignant as
their master at the insult which had been offered to
him, were proportionately active in resenting it.
In a moment the Scindee was on his back; in
another his ancles were lashed tight to the stout
staff supported upon two fellows' shoulders, and long
before the minute was over, four stout ruffians were
"quilting" the unfortunate's soles and toes, even as

---

* A literal translation of the common address to inferiors, " baba-sog."

upholsterers' boys in Italy beat out the stuffing of
old mattresses, whilst their master stood up ejaculat-
ing, *Wurin! Wurin!!* * with all the dignity of a
Kajjar. The Agha was in no mood to be merciful,
and it is a common practice among Persians when
you prescribe a sound-flogging, to make any one who
spares the sufferer share his fate.

When at length the Scindee had fainted from
pain and loss of blood, the Agha was graciously
pleased to deliver himself of a wave of the hand,
which the executioners understood to signify that a
quantum sufficit of chastisement had been administered.

" And what was he chastised for?"

What for? for the abominable crime of showing
his belief that child of man could possibly be so
audacious as to conceive the project of attacking
such a personage as Agha Khan.

Two hundred years ago, Mr. Bull, you would not
have put the question. Let us refer back to the
history of your own island for a proof. None will
do better than a short extract from old Andrew de
Wyntoun's " Orygynale Cronykil " of Scotland.

* " Strike!" The word is Turkish, a language preferred by the
present ruling family of Persia, who are Kajjar Turks, on account of its
severe and dignified sonorousness.

When David II., after nine or ten years' captivity
in the so-called merry England, was ransomed by his
nobles, he journeyed northward, and arrived with
the slenderest of retinues at Berwick, where

——— " Upon the morn when he
Should wend, till his counsel privy
The folk, as they were wont to do,
Pressed right rudely in thereto.
But he right suddenly can arrace
Out of a macer's hand a mace,
And said rudely, 'How do we now?'
Stand still, or the proudest of you
Shall on the head have with this mace !"

In the nineteenth century you are disposed to
think that the "just Kynge Davie" was guilty of a
gross outrage in threatening to crack the polls of
his subjects, who, after doing so much for, were
pressing forward to see and greet their ransomed
sovereign; and you cannot but wonder how the
priestly bard brings himself to justify his liege's
violence by a long encomium upon the subject of
" radure" (rigour) :—

" Radure in Prince is a good thing :
For, but radure, all governing
Shall all times but despised be."

In Scinde still, as in England whilome, if you do
not occasionally shake the bit in the animal's mouth,

and administer a severe twitch or two to remind him that he has a master, he is sorely apt to forget the fact, or to remember it with the intention of changing places with that master the first opportunity that presents itself.

But you have had time to bury such barbarisms in oblivion. When the late Pacha of Egypt was dying you wondered excessively what could be the use of a proclamation which threatened instant decapitation to any man that dared assert the ruler was defunct. We semi-orientals understood the object of it perfectly well. In many Eastern countries the moment the throne becomes vacant, all the *canaille* and *mauvais sujets* of the different cities, and all the wild tribes in their vicinity, begin to run riot, to rob, ravish, and plunder *à tort et à travers;* and the successor to the vacant seat of dignity, after probably a year's hard fighting, ending with a dearly bought victory, which enables him to blind a score or two of uncles, brothers, cousins, and other kinsmen, has to march an army against his own subjects, with the unpleasant necessity of diminishing their numbers by the axe, the cord, and the stake, and of injuring his revenue by leading a host of human locusts through the land.

However, to conclude my tale of Agha Khan:

Scarcely had the wretched Scindian's lacerated stumps been stuck in a neighbouring dunghill—the recognised treatment for the complaint under which he was labouring—when down came the Belochies upon Jerruck in the most ferocious and rapacious of moods. Finding no arrangements made to oppose them, they scaled the puddle parapet, dashed into the town, cut to pieces every beardless man* they met, and although they failed to secure the august person of the Agha, they did not fail to appropriate the contents of his cellar and harem. The potentate lost much valuable property in wines and other liquors. It was not before some weeks afterwards that he recovered his wives; and when he did, he did not appreciate the value of the goods in question.

Jerruck is about one hundred miles along the road from Kurrachee. We have now left behind Lar or Lower Scinde. This is Wicholo,† the "central region." You can feel that we are travelling northwards; the air becomes sensibly drier, and in the nights and mornings more biting. During the

---

* Young Persians, like the Turkish soldiery, generally shave the beard.

† Our geographers usually divide the province into two parts, Upper and Lower Scinde ; the point of demarcation being Halehkandi, a town situated a few miles north of Hyderabad. The natives, with more topographical correctness, distribute it into three districts.

summer season the mid-day heats are more violent, as the last breath of the sea breeze is exhaled upon the plain of Tattah.*

* Some will tell you it reaches Hyderabad : I cannot, however, say that I ever felt it north of Tattah.

CHAPTER XI.

KOTREE. — A COMEDY OF BAGGAGE-BEASTS. — THE
INTRENCHED CAMP—HYDERABAD. .

A SKETCH of the history and geography of the
country ?

No, Mr. Bull.   In the first place, the subjects
have been exhausted by a host of industrious Orien-
talists. Secondly, their failures in interesting you, and
the *per se* deadly uninteresting nature of the theme,
do imperatively forbid my making the attempt.

Oriental history,* sir, may be separated into two
forms of matter.   The ancient is a collection of
wildly imaginative and most unartful legends and
traditions, preserved or invented by individuals who
were like old Livy's authorities—

———— " for profound
And solid lying much renowned ; "

from the mighty mass of which dross and rubbish

* These remarks are mainly intended as a general character of
Oriental Historiography.

no workman less cunning than Niebuhr or Arnold could extract the smallest quantity of ore.

The chronicles of the times that range within authenticity, are masses of proper names connected by a string of adventure spun out with peculiar fineness — impartially told as the most unimportant events are, at least as diffusedly detailed as the most important—abounding in digressions so unskilfully managed that you must fail to discover when the author starts for or returns from his bye-way trip; prolix where they should be concise, and compendious where minuteness is desirable, full of the valueless facts of history, void of the invaluable philosophy of history, and generally deficient in all that highly educated Europe has determined to be the "duty of a wise and worthy writer of history."

As an instance: "In short, after the capture of Alor, the metropolis of the province, all the dependent states becoming tranquil, the people returned to their usual avocations, and felt grateful to Mohammed bin Kasim. He constituted Harun the son of Kais, the son of Rawah, the Asidi, governor of Alor, and with the dignity of Kazi he invested Musa, the son of Yakrib, the son of Tai, the son of Nashban, the son of Usman, the Sakufi; and he constituted Widah, the son of Ahmed, the Nejdi, commandant

of the city of Brahmanabad, and he gave the fort of
Rawur to Naubat, the son of Daraz, and the land of
Korah to Bazl, the son of Halawi.   Then he turned
towards Multan, and on his way arrived at the strong-
hold called Bahijeh, whence Kulsur, the son of
Chandra, the son of Silabij, a cousin of Dahir's, and
his enemy, came forth and tendered his allegiancè.
After that, they conquered the fort of Sakar and
left Attah the son of Jumahi to command it.   Then
seizing Multan and all its dependencies, forts, strongholds and other places, Kazimah the son of Abd-el-
Malik, the son of Tamim, was left at Mahpur, and
Daud, the son of Musa, the son of Walid, the Ham-
mami, being a trustworthy man, was appointed
governor of Multan."

Now Brahmanabad—a wrong name by the by *—
was one of the principal cities in Scinde, and the
fortress of Multan has ever been the "key of Western
India."   Yet the author dismisses them summarily
as he does unknown Rawur or obscure Bahijah.

The rhyming chroniclers — as amongst us in
ancient times there are poetic historians in the East
—may be characterised as a body of court flatterers,
who select for their uninteresting effusions, some

---

* Because the word is partly Sanscrit, partly Persian ; consequently,
not Scindian.

theme which sounds musical enough in the prince's ears to provoke his liberality.

Both, poetic and prosaic, are full of such "vehement, iterated, and unblushing" falsehoods that the perusal of their pages presently becomes a painful task.

And, finally, there is a fatiguing monotony in the very stuff of Oriental history. Invariably some humble hero, or small statesman raises himself in the world by his good sword, pen, or tongue. Either he or his son dethrones an effete dynasty, and with the full consent of the people, constitutes himself their rightful despot. In the course of three generations the new family grows old, imitates their predecessors, and produces nothing but a swarm of villains, cowards, and debauchees; the last of whom is, with rigid retributive justice, in due time dethroned by some other small statesman or humble hero. And so on.

The history and geography of Scinde in the olden time, are equally and exceedingly unsatisfactory.

The country contains few memorials of by-gone ages, and no monuments of antiquity from which we moderns may pick up gleanings of information. Hindoo writers are all but silent upon the subject, infinitely as it interests their race. The Moslem accounts of it, commence in the first century of the Hijrah. Concerning the mighty torrent of Sanscrit-speaking people who, three thousand years before our race, poured from the bleak hills and blooming valleys of Central Asia, to deluge the plains of India, nothing but the bare fact has descended to us. Between the trips which the Macedonians made down the Sindhu,* and the march of the Moslem up its banks there is a hopeless blank of eleven centuries. Though passed and repassed by each countless horde that hurried to enrich and enjoy itself in—

"The land of fatal wealth and charms,"

not an inscription or even a stone remains in the country to mark a single circumstance. The province is a sloping surface of silt and sand, through which the Indus cuts its varying way with a facility that passes description. A few feet of brickwork built up in the bed might diverge the stream into another channel, cause the decline and downfall of a metropolis and twenty towns, convert a region of gardens into a silt desert, and tranfer plenty and population to what a month before was a glaring waste.

As regards the ancient course of the Lower Indus,

* The Indus.

infinite has been the speculation, the theorisation, the dissertation, the argument, and the contradiction upon this much vexed, and now most vexatious subject. But listen to the voice of reason, as proceeding from one Dr. Lord.[*]

"The river discharges 300 cubic feet of mud in every second of time; or a quantity which in seven months would suffice to form an island 42 miles long, 27 miles broad, and 40 feet deep; which (the mean depth of the sea on the coast being five fathoms), would consequently be elevated 10 feet above the surface of the water. Any person who chooses to run out this calculation to hundreds and thousands of years will be able to satisfy himself that much may be done by causes at present in action towards manufacturing Deltas."

*   *   *   *

This morning we pass over the long flat which occupies the right bank of the river. The country looks less barren and desolate; there are fewer heaps of drifted sand in sight, and there is some verdure besides that of Euphorbia, Asclepias, Parkinsonia, Capparis, Tamarisk, and wild Indigo. We acknowledge the presence of fields—little square places, in lines of raised clay, to contain and distribute the

* In his "Memoir on the Plain of the Indus."

fertilising fluid drawn up by the Persian wheels from the cuts and canals that branch off from the main stream. At this season there is nothing but the stubble of maize and millet, wheat and barley, upon the hard, dry ground. But large scattered villages stud the plain, and the inhabitants look healthy and well-doing compared with the pallid, squalid, meagre wretches in the Delta, who after every sentence complain of " Ghano Tap." *

To-day's encamping ground is an execrable one, close to an expanse of ribbed sand, and slimy pools, whence the waters of the inundation have just retired; and far enough from any town or village to prevent our procuring what man need never want in the East—milk. We must endure the discomfort as we best can. To-morrow we reach Kotree.

*   *   *   *

There lies our destination—a thick grove of date trees clothing the right side of the stream, with a few scattered bungalows built in and about it, a dirty bazaar of mud huts, thatched with palmetto leaves, crowded with dirtier natives, and a number of small flat-bottomed steamers anchored below the bank. This is the chief station of the Indus Flotilla, a branch of the Indian Navy or Bombay Marine,

---

* A terrible fever.

appropriated to the navigation of the river whose name it bears. For the protection of the stores and the defence of Kotree, there exists, as you may see, a small fort, of oriental or mediæval shape—one of those straight-curtained, ditchless, round-towered glacis-less things, under the walls of which is dead ground enough for a couple of regiments to dine in perfect safety. It has a habit of falling, too; there are no white ants hereabouts, it is said, but the saltpetre in the sun-dried bricks ruins buildings quite as quickly as those Lilliputian miners could do.

You now know the discomfort of arriving at a civilised place. On the road, we sometimes find "Traveller's Bungalows;" here, as at Kurrachee, Hyderabad, and Sukkur—in fact, wherever they are most required—there is certainly none. This is a general rule throughout Western India; you are justified in remarking that the sooner it is broken through the better. Our servants having done their duty, as they imagine, in pitching our tents, start for the bazaar, leaving a "cook-boy" to serve up our breakfasts, and a single horsekeeper to wait upon both our nags. Probably they will not return for half the day; and when they do, it will be in a state of pronounced inebriation, quarrelling, fighting, and manifesting many other unpleasant consequences of sacrificing to Oriental Bacchus. In the jungle, our minds are at rest; in the camp they are excited, restless, uneasy. There are *compatriotes* within hail; there is a library, a billiard-room, a mess, an acquaintance or two, ladies; but how are we to leave the tents? As the place is somewhat civilised, so it is literally full of plunderers: we shall be lucky if even our presence prevents their depredations.

Opportunely appears a little illustration of the Kotree's character, as by me drawn. A thief has been taken for judgment before the Deputy Collector and magistrate; his case was entered into and disposed of in about ten minutes—law proceedings here are not lengthy just now—and sentence passed upon him, he has been led out for punishment.

The fellow's brawny back—he is an African slave —is bared; his arms and legs are tightly lashed to one of the wooden posts which support the official's verandah. Then a belted Peon,* scourge in hand, works at the black shagreen with all his might. The dignitary himself is there, with a jockey cap and a cheroot in his mouth, to superintend the chastisement, and give a " moral effect " to the scene. But though he urges the willing lasher, and there are signs that the discipline is severe enough,

---

* An attendant upon official personages in India.

the slave scarcely takes the trouble of flinching, and
when at times he howls, it is rather in derision than
in deprecation.   His friends and fellow-countrymen,
coalheavers to the Flotilla, stand in a crowd, laughing
and chatting together: they have tasted English
liberty for a few months, and are now impudent as
London cads or an old noblewoman's pet courier.

* * * *

The sooner we leave Kotree the better.   Our
camels and horses, raw animals, are not much used
to the passage of rivers : there will be many a *scena*
before the ferry lands us on the opposite bank.

First come the camel-men—two mountaineers,
four feet and a half high, and almost as broad as
they are long; bandy-legged little monsters, with
broad faces, flat features, swart skins, shaggy beards,
and scowls that seem to engross the business of
their countenances—to swear that their beasts never
have entered a boat, and, *par conséquence*, that they
never will.   Not noticing the fallacy of the *ergo*, we
briefly reply that they must, and thus the prologue
concludes.

Opens act number one, with a camel-fight.   The
beasts are huddled in a herd upon the bank, and,
not knowing what to do, a pair of the biggest spon-
taneously engage in single combat.   They are very

like Germans in one point; usually most placid and imperturbable, now that they are excited, they become very devils, biting and bellowing, pushing and kicking, with an activity that amazes, and a violence that startles one. Act the first will conclude, after many a shifting scene, with a tremendous drubbing upon the heads, ribs, and quarters of the principal performers by the clubs of the enraged *propriétaires*.

Act the second opens with a "lively scene"— embarkation. The stage is thus decorated for the *tableau*.

A quantity of earth is taken from the bank, and so disposed, that a very inclined plane may lead down to the water's edge. Then an animal is induced to advance; his driver, standing in the ferry-boat, hauls at the nose strings, whilst the beast, his tail borne pug-dog fashion, and his vocal organs in fullest activity, stretches his long neck, and lengthens all his limbs with a pertinacity and a determination not to move, over which nothing but a perfect storm of blows on flank and haunch can prevail. At times, holding back and roaring, now with some reason : at times slipping and plunging, the patient at length reaches the gap that separates bank from boat. Another furious struggle. More obstinacy. Nothing will persuade him to raise his foreleg and plant foot

upon the ferry. He kicks and flounders, now falling
into the water himself, now pushing half a dozen of
his assailants into it.   At last, a cord is tied round
the ancle of the near arm; four men drag at it. A
dozen,—the mob of idlers, gathered around us is
beginning to take an interest in the struggle,—push
his buttocks with both hands, and hammer at any
vacant space with their sticks and fists, screaming,
commanding, abusing, and retorting, till main force
drives him boggling, stamping, scrambling, and
floundering into the boat, where his nostrils are
twitched and his long shins are kicked, till he finds
it advisable to kneel in all humility. With our ten
camels, this part of the play will take four hours.

Act the third and last. The horses appear. Most
of them hop cleverly over the ferry's side, and take
up the position allotted to them as readily as if
entering their stalls. But that surly Affghan yaboo *
of yours is not accustomed to such a luxury of travel,
and perversely obstinate as an animal of that very
Moslem nation might be expected to prove himself,
he will have nothing to do with the strange refine-
ment. This our men can easily correct. To prevent
his lashing out, they tie a rope to one of his forelegs
and pull it till the member in question assumes the

* A pony.

legitimate and classical, equestrian statue-form. Then two horse-keepers, seizing a long pole, apply the middle of it to the recusant's hinder region, and shove till he has nothing to do but either to fall headlong upon his nose, or to jump into the boat. He is sure to choose the latter alternative, and after five or six repetitions of the exercise, it will become quite familiar to him.

Concluding with the epilogue—a largess of coppers to the crowd, we also cross. Observe the force of the current, how it carries our conveyance down the stream. You may see its migratory habits also: witness that gentleman's horse, once twenty yards from the bank, now seen *in ispaccato* one half in, the other out of, the river. This is the Entrenched Camp: the field-works, which surround it, have given it a name. That humble building, somewhat in the form of a six dozen claret-chest, magnified and white-washed, with the barren court on the east, and a garden, grove, and sundry small bungalows to the south, is the Agency, still memorable for the gallant defence made by a company of British soldiers * against a host of enraged Belochies.

It is about three miles from the Entrenched Camp

* The Light Company of H.M.'s 22d Regiment, commanded by Captain Conway.

to Hyderabad, along a dusty, rutty slip of plain, called a road, planted with trees, which, if watered and not eaten by goats, will shadow the next generation, across the normal southern Scinde country, a network of canals and watercourses spread over straggling crops of thorns and fir plants. The approach to the town is picturesque. We emerge from a little grove : on the left, is a hill crowned by a native fortification, with the gaudy shrine of Shah Mekkai, and a cluster of houses at its foot. To our right, the burial-ground, a square enclosure, above whose walls appear the tops of many tombs, and in front, the road that separates the town from its protecting fort, winds up the steep and stony hill.

Hyderabad, lately the capital of Scinde, occupies the centre of a little island, formed by the Indus and one of its multitudinous branches, the Fulailee. The site of the city is a low chain of limestone hills rising a few feet above the alluvial plain : the fancied advantages to be derived from commanding ground, probably pointed it out as a fit place for a settlement in ancient times.

The town contains nothing that merits description. It is a mass of flat-roofed houses and sloping-roofed huts, separated by narrow, dark, dusty, or muddy streets and alleys, with here and there a dome and a minaret, a crowded bazaar, and a heap of ruins. The principal habitations are two or many-storied, extensive structures, with naked, glassless windows placed jealously high up, and dependent courtyards carefully invested with stiff-looking walls of puddle or unbaked bricks. Almost all tenements boast of verandahs.

Except in the market-places, there is little or no bustle in the city, and, as we ride through it, the people, accustomed to the presence of Europeans, scarcely stand to stare at the endemic " calamity," * to whose horrors habit has hardened them. The ladies know it is useless to beckon us, the fakirs have learned the fallacy of begging from us; the curs have forgotten to bark at us, and the infant population to taunt us with infidelity. Every here and there we see a knot of seapoys chaffering in the bazaar, and officers' servants sauntering about in the luxury of indolence,—we feel that we are in a " Station."

The Fort of Hyderabad, conspicuous from afar by its lofty round bastion or watch-tower,—a windmill-like structure of huge proportions, erroneously supposed to have been the treasury of the Ameers,—is built upon the southern spur of the long, narrow, rocky ridge on which the city stands. Its form is

* In Arabic and Persian, " balá," any strange portent.

an irregular oval, about three quarters of a mile in circumference. It is girt by lofty, crumbling, ill-burnt, brick revêtements, thick at the base, thin at the crest, and supporting inside a quantity of earth, piled upon the natural rock. They look as if a few rounds of grape would level them with the plain,—an appearance the reverse of deceitful,—this boasted stronghold of the boastful Talpur, being one of the weakest amongst the strong-seeming fortresses of this bit of Asia. On the northern side, a trench separates the citadel from the town: it is crossed by a bridge, leading to one of those perversely intricate gateways that have always yielded to a *coup de main:* every-where else is level ground. There are few embra-sures for large guns. No angles, no outworks: the spear-head battlement of Persia runs along the crest to shelter matchlock-men, and down the height of the wall are lines of—what our Irânian neighbours call damágheh—nostrils—apertures, which act as drains and loopholes combined.

The citadel was at once the place of defence, the treasury, and the palace of the native rulers. The interior resembles a small town, a *Haute-ville;* it has its promenade round the ramparts, its streets and thoroughfares, its squares and guards, its mosques, its shops and booths, its lines and its barracks.

Many of the houses, once the abodes of royalty, are spacious and convenient, especially since glass doors and lattices have started into being.

The ground plan of a Hyderabad palace is this. You enter by a low door—more generally by a doorway without a door—opening from a narrow lane into a quadrangular court-yard; on your right is the private chapel, a low wall subtended by a stuccoed floor; opposite you, the stables; on the left are the kitchen, offices, and servants' huts; the fourth side is occupied by the body of the house. The dwelling-place consists of an open verandah, with pillars, and a parapet in front. The state or men's apartments meet you as you enter; the ladies' rooms are under arrest behind them. Dwarf doors connect the different divisions, and the whole interior is purposely made as dark as possible, to obviate glare and secure privacy. Some rooms are elegantly stuccoed and elaborately painted with coloured arabesques, somewhat like our stencilling, that gives a Moorish look to the scene; in the ceilings of the richest houses there must have been at one time a quantity of gilding and expensive ornaments. In the inner walls are a number of niches, and when I first saw them not a few holes; for the Ameers and their courtiers being taken by surprise by the result of " Meeanee," deposited *more Asiatico* their gold bars and jewels in boxes, which they buried under the thresholds, in the walls of the houses, and in other places which a Western would seldom visit with the hope of finding a treasure. This fact become generally known, caused abundant harmless excitement among the conquerors. Europeans as well as natives did nothing for six months but diligently rap with staves every foot of stucco to infer by the sound whether the spot was hollow, and, consequently, worth the trouble of breaking into.

We are well in the region of ventilators; you see them on every roof—diminutive screens of masonry, forming acute angles with the apertures over which they project. The wind rushing down a passage in the wall, enters the room by a slit on the level of the floor, generally, in these days, cooling a bottle of pale ale as it passes. There is one great disadvantage in these "breeze-catches," as they are called; in boisterous weather they make your domicile a dust-hole. Unfortunately for its conquerors, Hyderabad is not far north enough to know the luxury of Tah-khanas—underground rooms, in which you may pass the awful length of a summer's day, dozing as coolly and comfortably as if you were on the Rhine or in the Pyrenees.

The ramparts command an extensive view of the neighbouring country. Many villages, sparkling like cornelians amidst the emerald green of the Neem* tree, stud the wide plain of black dust. You can trace on one side the course of the Fulailee river, winding through the wintry, barren flat; on the other, the broad Indus, with its buttress of rocky hill in the background. Before you lies a dense array of houses, here sinking into suburbs that fine off into gardens, there bristling over the ridge till it ends in the stray waste, where the lines of the soldiery and the houses of the Collectors are. Those distant domes of glittering white marble are the sepulchres of certain Kalhora Princes. There is a race-course, as usual in India; and I suppose, at some time or other, there will be a church. Beneath you is the burial-ground;—how fearfully full it is, considering the few years that has populated it ! *There* appears one of the causes of its repletion—a sheet of water, the remnant of last summer's inundation, thick as a horse-pond below, beautifully verdant above, on a bed of slimy mud, amidst banks of dark purple mire.

Is it not wonderful,—I beg no pardon for digressing, —sir, that in such a Sierra Leone as this, more care is

* The *Melia Azadirachta.*

not taken to secure health? At Kurrachee, within a few hundred yards of the cantonment, the corpses of fifty camels are allowed to lie and fester, and feed the jackalls, and poison the air, as if a little more death were really wanting. Tattah is a mass of filth, and here we have this miasma-breeding pool as close to the walls as a junior ensign could desire. How impress upon this Anglo-Indian mind the paramount importance of drainage and cleanliness? Were I ever to command a station, no Dutch village, no Chandernagore,* should be more scrupulously, more priggishly clean. Woe to the man that then throws his dead cat over his neighbour's hedge! Alas for him that allows his unwashed Portuguese cook to empty the surplus of the kitchen into the pit that now acts sink and sewer!

Walking round the battlements we see, half way down the steps that lead to the wicket, a large well or two cut deep in the solid rock. There is something remarkable in their appearance; the natives, as is the wont of savages when anything, natural or artificial, strikes them, assign to them a highly fanciful origin. These are the works of demon hands, excavations made in the stone at a time when an

---

* A little French settlement in Eastern India, celebrated for cleanliness, and, consequently, remarkable for healthfulness.

idol worshipper was Lord of Nirunkot,* for the fell purpose of incarcerating that holy personage whose mortal remains rest in yonder shrine.

Here is the legend :—

There was errantry in the East when Islam arose. Combative individuals with brains about equal to those of the animals they bestrode; churchmen militant with the thews and sinews of baggage camels, "furious knights" like him of More Hall, who

> "Could wrestle, play at quarterstaff, kick, cuff, and huff;
>   Call son of a dog, do any kind of thing,"

composed an order almost as honourable and as honoured as any in the host of our western chivalry. Only instead of devoting themselves to bemaul all who could or would not acknowledge the personal superiority of a Lady Bellisance or a Dulcinea, they pricked o'er the plain pounding the skulls and piercing the bodies of those wretches whose opaque minds refused to be enlightened by the dazzling glories of the apothegm—"Mohammed is the Prophet of the Lord."

It is, however, pleasurable to observe that these same heroes were at times by no means insensible to

---

* The "Fort of Nirun"—Hyderabad—anciently so called after its pagan founder.

the tender passion; indeed, in many cases they appear to have made love at least as furiously as they fought, and seldom to have slain a notorious pagan without carrying off, converting, and espousing his fair widow or daughter; of which the veritable history of Mohammed the Brave, popularly called Shah Mekkai* is a good example.

As the Brave, one of the Ashab or disciple-companions of Ali, Mohammed's son-in-law, after quitting Mecca, his birth-place, was wandering about the world in quest of adventure, he happened to be benighted in the vicinity of Hyderabad—then a very hotbed of heathenry. And the Beebee Nigar, the daughter of Nirun, and a lady of Amazonian habits, seeing a man in strange clothing cooking a supper of her father's black partridges, approached, and indulged him in his hobby by challenging him incontinently to the duello. The style of combat proposed was the rude and primitive form of the "noble art" as practised of yore by the Lion-hearted King and the Copmanhurst Slasher; one party being desired to deal a goodly buffet to the other, who, being forbidden to stop or to slip down, was in his turn requested to repay the compliment. The Brave had the first chance; but although his arm

* The "King," (i. e., great man, holy personage), of or from Mecca.

usually could fell an ox, and his fingers could rip up
a shirt of mail as easily as you, Mr. Bull, would tear
a yard of calico, on this occasion he was obliged to
own that his hand had lost all its power.

Then the lady unhelmed her face.   Then of course
the Brave fell in love with the lady, and then—such
things are managed with admirable speed in oriental
and tropical lands,—the lady and the Brave instantaneously plighted their troth and swore to become
man and wife as soon as possible.

Unfortunately for the case of True Love *versus*
a Certain Proverb, they parted—the Beebee returning home till her admirer travelled to Mecca, and
obtained permission from his commanding officer Ali,
effectually, as Sir C— N— saith, to "ruin himself
for the service," that is, to lead home a spouse.   Some
of the lady's attendants having observed her little
flirtation with the foreign man, lost not a moment
in informing their master of the same; and the
infidel king, in order to obviate the possible perils of
such proceedings, determined at once to find a
suitable *partie* for his *demoiselle*.

In despair, the fair one started a camel-man with
an order to pursue the Brave, and a message that
would recall him.   Bahadur, that individual, succeeded in his attempts, and the two, as they were

hurrying towards Nirunkot, were joined by the valiant Ali, on his celebrated Rosinante, Zu'l Zenah, "the lord of wings."

They arrived at the fort in time to hear the sound of nuptial music, and to see crowds in gay attire gathered to celebrate the nuptials of their princess. Touching coincidence!

Mall Mohammed, now desperate in his turn, left Ali hid in a garden, and disguising himself as a pagan, penetrated into the fortress, and made his way to the abode of royalty. But Nirun being, as might be expected, a magician as well as a wicked heathen, soon discovered who the intruder was, by the sudden stopping of the music. So, summoning all his attendant devils, he threw the Brave into yonder well, and rolled a stone which no fifty men in these degenerate days could move, over the flesh-pot as a lid.

It was now Ali's turn to act. He waited till evening came on. Then, anxious and impatient, he followed his *protégé's* example in entering the fort disguised, but, instead of confronting the old pagan, with superior sagacity, he walked straight into the young lady's boudoir, and then hid himself under the bridal couch.

Events followed in rapid succession. First a little

conjugal squabble, in which the lady informed her
lord that though her hand might legally be his,
her heart was solely "another's." Secondly, the
sudden slaughter of that lord, who being a dull man
was at once placed *hors de combat* by the valiant
Ali's *miséricorde*. Thirdly, a rapid dialogue between
the dame and her deliverer, when the former informed
the latter, that the devoted lover was imprisoned in
the Devil's Well. Fourthly, the liberation of the
captive; and, lastly, the "bolting" of the three
Faithfuls, with a pack of infidel hounds at their
heels.

They gallopped over the plain; they halted not at
the bank of the Indus; they—

——— "forded the river and clomb the high hill,"

(called Hala) all that night, and as the morn, not dressed
in a russet mantle, but in a very crimson velvet, like
a portly dowager at a Bath Assembly, began to
expose her well rouged face to the *beau monde*, they
had almost reached a place of safety in the Sulayman
mountains.

There was manifested a beautiful effect of piety on
the part of the three fugitives. As I said, a posse of
heathens was upon their track, eager as the wolves
that coursed Mazeppa's steed, or the bailiffs which

Christian creditors send in search of their debtor-brethren; in a word, death or captivity, within a few yards, pursued them. But for such paltry ephemeral mundane considerations could they, think you, neglect their morning prayers? Certainly not!

Consequently the brief conclusion of the tale is a highly pathetic one. The lady was martyred, whilst the trace of genuflection was on her shins, and five minutes afterwards, her lover shared her fate. Only as he had lost a wife in prospect, he appears to have been very ferocious, and to have died hard, fighting to the last, rampantly valorous.

Ali was obliged to content himself with killing a few tens of thousands, with routing the host, and with cutting off that arch-infidel's, the old gentleman's, head; upon which he turned his steed Mecca-ward, and quitted for ever the "tragical scene."

* * * *

Here we remain a month or so, Mr. John Bull, to prepare your mind and body for the trips which I have in store for you.

CHAPTER XII.

THE HINDOOS OF SCINDE—THEIR RASCALITY AND THEIR PHILOPROGENITIVENESS.

THE native population of Scinde—"the extreme western limit to which Hindooism in these days extends"—is composed of Moslems and Polytheists. The former, being nearly four times the more numerous, are the great mass of the community; whereas the latter are, with few exceptions, the trading members of the social body.

As has before been said, at the time of the Arab invasion (A.D. 710) Scinde, like Affghanistan, Mooltan, and the regions that lie to the north of it, was one of the strongholds of Hindooism. It is probable that most of the ancient families that survived the capture of their country, migrated to escape the persecution of their deistical conquerors, eastwards to Jesulmere, and the adjacent provinces, where their faith was the religion of the state. The present Hindoo population of Scinde consists principally of castes that originally immigrated from the Panjab and Cutch; this their language, dress, manners, and appearance amply testify, though now, naturalised in the country, all but their learned men have forgotten the story of their origin.

Late as the eighteenth century, the Hindoos of Scinde, we are informed by a traveller, were ten times more numerous than the rival sect. Hindooism, however, like Judaism, has ever been an eyesore to the Moslem, and the means which he adopts to remove it, although violent and unjust, are not the less efficacious. In Persia, for instance, the Jew is popularly supposed to sacrifice a Moslem child on certain occasions. Whenever a boy disappears, a hue and cry is raised; requiring an object, it directs itself against the persecuted body: their houses are attacked and plundered, they are dragged before the least impartial of judges, their oaths and their testimony are regarded as the whisperings of the wind, and the scene ends either with the question, or an order to admit the accused into the ranks of the Faithful. And when once the proselyte's foot has crossed the threshold of the Mosque all hope of retreat is permanently cut off—the punishment of apostacy being as certain as it is tremendous.

In Scinde the same cause—bigotry, partially

modified, operated to work the downfall of heathenism, which, had we not taken the country, would probably not have outlived the century.

The Talpurs, the last reigning family, came down from the hills of Beloochistan, and settled upon the sultry plains below, first as the disciples, then as the feudal followers of the saintly race which they afterwards dethroned. Years spent in the enervating climate of the valley dulled the bravery and hardihood of the mountaineer, but left him all his natural ignorance, and bigotry, and cruelty. A Talpur chief of the last generation refused even to place a watch for repair in the hands of an accused but-parast, or idol-worshipper.

In the West there are many, in the East few exceptions to the Arabs' political axiom,

"The prince is the religious pattern of his people;"

and here the subjects, seeing the sovereign's propensity for persecution, copied the pattern as closely as they could.

No Hindoo ventured to pronounce the name of the village Allahyara jo Tando,* because of the holy dissyllable that commences it; he could not touch a paper written in the Arabic language, because that

* The village of "God's-friend"—the latter word being the proper name of some Moslem.

character was the character of the Koran;* nor dared
he to open a Moslem book in his mother tongue, the
Scindee, for fear of being seen to peruse the inceptive
formula, "In the name of Allah, the compassionate,
the merciful." It was always in the power of two
Moslems to effect the conversion of a Pagan by
swearing that they saw him at a cockfight on Friday,
that he pronounced, in their presence, the word
Mohammed, or even that he had used some such
ambiguous phrase as "I will go with thee."† Sometimes circumcision was made the penalty of crime, as
where a Hindoo banyan, or shopkeeper, falsely
accused a seapoy of Dr. Burnes's guard of robbing
him, the Ameer at once ordered the cazee to do his
work upon the offender. Nothing easier than to
make a Moslem in those days. The patient was
taken before the judge, where, after being stripped of
his old clothes, the ceremonial ablution was duly
performed, and he was invested in the garments that
denote the Faithful. A crowd of jubilants then
chaired him to the Mosque; prayers were recited over
him, he was directed thrice to repeat Mohammed's
creed—and, if he did it fluently, a minor miracle

* Rather, I should say, supposed to have been the character by Oriental
ignoramuses in palæography.

† The Moslem Scindians in the present day deny these assertions; the
Hindoos exaggerate them; and we simply believe them.

was got up—next came circumcision, the eating a bit
of beef, a change of name, a feast, and, lastly, a very
concise course of instruction in the ceremonial part
of the new faith.

But the consequences of becoming a proselyte
extended far enough. Islam, like many other faiths,
professing to respect the convert, despises and dis-
trusts him.   In Scinde he was compelled to enter a
certain caste—one of no high degree—to marry in
it, and to identify himself with the mongrel mass it
contained.   He rarely rose to fortune or distinction,
and seldom could command the respect of his
co-religionists, who doubted the reality of his attachment to the strange faith, and his hankering after
the old idolatry.   If, on the other hand, conscience
or discontent drove the proselyte into a land where
he might recant without danger, or if an opportunity,
such as our seizure of the country, presented itself,
the return to Hindooism, when practicable, was
accompanied with many a disagreeable.   In some
towns, where Polytheists are few, and cannot afford
to reject a wealthy and influential applicant, large
presents to Brahmans, rigid expiatory penances, and
a pilgrimage, were the price of readmission to the
religion of their forefathers. But this was not always
possible.   There are many places where the recanter

is not received; he has eaten the flesh of the cow, and has drank impure water; for the rest of his life, therefore, he must dwell in the house of his family, an outcast, a defiled man, whose touch, like the leper's of yore, is pollution; separated from his wife, powerless over his children, with nothing but the dreary prospect held out by his gloomy faith to console him under a life of uncommon trials.

With the vulgar the excitement of making one convert bred a desire to make another and another. When opportunities were rare, they were obliged to content themselves with robbing the Pagans : Friday —the Moslem Sunday—being generally selected as the time for these small St. Bartholomew displays. There were few towns in which a Hindoo could safely leave his house between Thursday evening and Saturday morning.

All the which the persecuted race endured doggedly in the *spes finis*. Sulking under the sabre sway of their rulers, they revenged themselves indirectly ; the lower orders by grinding the faces of the poor Moslems, the upper classes by acquiring power to be abused, by fomenting intestine and family feuds, by corrupting the principal officers of the state, and by sadly confusing all ideas of *éntente cordiale* with neighbouring and allied kingdoms. Thus, despicable and despised as they were, they failed not to prove themselves essentially dangerous.

Superiority of intellect was on their list. The Hindoo mind is a mathematical one; the Moslem's, generally speaking,* notably deficient in the power of mastering the exact sciences. This I believe to be the first cause of a phenomenon which attracts every observing eye in India, namely, that when the Polytheist and the Monotheist meet on at all equal terms, the former either ruins, or subjects to himself the latter. Other qualities accompany this form or constitution of the brain in the worshipper of Brahma. He is a dark and deep-seeing plotter, an admirable eventualist where anything villainous is the event: what land but India could have kept up Thuggee for centuries?—what was the Vehme of Germany, or the Fidawiyat of Hasan Sabah,† in organisation, combination, or duration, compared with it? He is remarkable for passive courage, in suffering braver than any woman: he will inflict injuries upon himself with the *sang froid* of a Leæna, provided you hold out to him the one inducement—wealth. With the money for his rent, or his debt concealed about

* The exceptions being some rare individuals amongst the Turks, Persians, Arabs, and Moors.

† Or Sayyah—for about his name annalists still differ—the Grand Master of the Assassins, and organiser of that remarkable order.

his person, to be produced when things are going too
far, he will allow himself to be suspended by his
thumbs or his heels till he faints; he will shriek
under the lash, swearing that he has not a pice, and
he will inhale finely powdered cayenne with all the
endurance, but very little of the stoicism, of a North
American Indian. His constancy requires nothing
but a cause to dignify it. Such is his passive courage.
At the same time place a weapon in his hand and
point to the bristling breach—desire him to charge
up to a gun like an Affghan or a Turk, he will look
at you, remonstrate, hang back, turn tail : this is
not his courage.* Finally he is parsimonious, a lean
half-naked wretch, with lacs at his command, living
on coarse bread and sugar-arrack, when a Moslem
with a few thousand rupees would be faring sump-
tuously, and emptying his purse upon silks and satins,
horses and dancers. Nor is this thriftiness by any
means a despicable quality: it goes hand in hand
with indefatigable industry.

At last the Hindoo arts prevailed, as might be
expected, over the strong arm. The younger Talpur
Ameers, the sons and nephews of the original Char
Yar, or the four friends and brothers who expelled

---

* I am speaking of the Scinde Hindoo, not of the Sikh, the Rajput, the
Nair, and other races which are educated, if I may use the expression, to
active courage.

the Kalhora dynasty from Scinde, acknowledged
their utter inability to dispense with heathens in
managing their miserable territory—a score of them
governed a country about the extent of England—
and in collecting their paltry revenue,—the total
produce of the province was not greater than the
income of a British nobleman of the second class.
The princes had degenerated from the hardy savage
virtues of temperance, sobriety, and morality affected
by their progenitors; they required for pleasure the
time demanded by business, and willingly intrusted
to the hands of Hindoos—most unjust stewards—the
management of their estates, and, in some cases, of
their subjects.

The worshipper of Brahma eminently possesses
the peculiarity usually attributed to Scotchmen—
the habit of carrying out in practice what all people
admit in theory—that "blood is thicker than water."
He no sooner establishes himself upon a firm footing
than he extends a helping hand to his family generally, even to his cousins twenty degrees removed.
Nor does he stop here.   Relations may be expended
—the "caste-brother," as he is called, cannot.   Thus
the rulers of Scinde were soon surrounded by a host
of civil officers, revenue collectors, secretaries, and
scribes, all of the same persuasion, all playing into

one another's hands, and all equally determined to aggrandise themselves, their family, and their race, no matter by what means. The result of this almost unopposed combination was that the princes, notwithstanding their powers of life and death, the "she-cat" * and circumcision, were never safe from frauds so barefaced that it moves our wonder to hear them told.

*   ᴛ   ᴛ   *.

Of the four great divisions that compose the pure Indian family, here we find but three—the Brahman, the Waishya (trader), and the Shudra, or servile man. The second, the royal and military caste, is in Scinde, as elsewhere, of doubtful faith and origin: every Sikh, even were he the son of a sweeper, assumes to himself the title of Kshatriya. The social position of the race prevents their putting forth that multitude of outcast branches which in India spring up from the transgression, voluntary or involuntary, of a single arbitrary religious ordinance.

The Scinde Brahman is by no means a correct specimen of his far-famed class. His diet is most inaccurate. Although he avoids beef and fowls, he will eat fish; also the flesh of wild birds and certain

---

* The billi or "she-cat," was a native instrument of torture, furnished with claws to tear the flesh of the questioned.

meats—such as venison, kid, and mutton; he shrinks not from the type of creation, an onion, and allows himself the forbidden luxury of strong waters. Instead of confining himself, as he should do, to the study of his grammar and his Scriptures, to his prayers and to his pastoral duties, he may be seen bending over the ledger, squatting on a counter, or exercising the command of a kitchen. When we first took the country, Brahmans owned to me that Brahmans sometimes actually married widows; but of late years, after being soundly rated by the sea-poys, whom they respect, these irregular unions have become rare amongst them.

There are two principal families of priests in Scinde—the Pokarno and the Sarsat. The former are supposed to have immigrated from Upper India; they worship Vishnu, the second person of the Hindu Triad; support themselves by a knowledge of Sauscrit, judicial astrology, and ceremonial law; marry in their own caste, and claim from their pontifical brethren a superiority which the others admit by receiving the " water from their hands." The Sarsat, or Sarsudh,* are worshippers of Shiva, the Destroyer: in education, appearance and manners, they exactly resemble the votaries of Vishnu.

* Properly Sáraswatiya, from the Saraswati river.

Knowledge amongst Scinde Brahmans means a proficiency in the simpler parts of Sanscrit grammar, and sufficient mastery over the language to understand oft-read works upon astrology, magical formula, and the volumes that contain the intricate practice of their faith. Some few have perused the Bhagawat, one of the fourteen religious poems called the Puranas, and here and there an individual has had the industry to form a superficial acquaintance with the Sanhita or Summary of the Yajur or White Veda. The increased facility for travelling to distant lands with a possibility of return, has of late years induced several Brahmans to venture far from the banks of the Indus, to wander amidst the classic shades of Kasi,* and to sit in the colleges of Calcutta: the extent of their acquirements proves that the race is by no means deficient in power of intellect. Few of the priestly order, except when engaged in commerce, know anything of the Persian language: it seems they consider it a profane study of erotic verses and "light literature," tales ill-suited to the gravity of a churchman and a scholar. But they have little objection to the compositions or even the tenets of that mild heretic Nanak Shah, the apostle of the Sikhs, principally, I presume, because the

* Benares.

mass of his followers praise and honour, revere and fee, the Brahmans.

The Brahman in Scinde shaves his head, leaving a single lock upon the poll; he removes the beard, and induces the moustaches to droop heavily over his mouth, in order to distinguish them from the hairy honors of the Moslem's lip. Upon his forehead he places a horizontal or a perpendicular mark indifferently.* His dress is generally that of a common Sahukar, or trader,—that is to say, a white or red turban,† a cotton coat with a short body and flowing skirts, a cloth, generally salmon-coloured, with an ornamental edge, wound round the waist, a shawl or sheet thrown loosely over the shoulders, and slippers of anything but of leather. In his hand is a sandal-wood rosary of twenty-seven grains; and constant habit has endowed him with the power of muttering and telling his beads mechanically. A few Sarsat Brahmans dress in the style affected by the Amils or Revenue officers: the Pokarno, however, consider the costume unclerical, and eschew it accordingly.

Of the Wani, Banyan or trader caste, there are five great families in this country, the Lohana, the

---

* Whereas in India the perpendicular Tilak as it is called, distinguishes the adorer of the Preserver, from the worshipper of the Destroyer.

† The Pokarno preferring the red, the Sarsat, the white, headgear.

Bhatia, the Sehta, those called Waishya,* and the Panjabi. According to the wont of Hindooism, each division is split into a number of insignificant bodies, who have their proper names derived from their place of residence, or peculiarities of dress and appearance, their furious *esprit de corps*, and their violent jealousies of one another, when the absence of a common foe allows them to indulge in the luxury of hatred, malice, and all uncharitableness.†

Divided according to their occupations the Scinde Banyans are of two classes. The ignorant multitude employs itself generally in commerce, sometimes in cultivation; the select few become officers under government, and take the title of Amil.

The Scinde trader has lived so long amongst and in subjection to the stranger, that he has unconsciously but very palpably emancipated himself from much of the galling bondage of a faith which fears progress as much as destruction. Tempted by the

* The word " Waishya " properly meaning the third or trading class of Hindoos, is here used in a limited sense to signify operatives and mechanics, opposed to merchants and shopkeepers.

† Most significant too, are some of their taunts. For instance, the Lohana, in general, say of the Khudawadi, one of their subdivisions :—

" *Khudawadi Khuda* khe ghere wanjan"—
The Khudawadi deceive the Almighty.—

A bad pun, but a sharp cut at the excessive cunning of that race.

hope of wealth, he has wandered far and wide from his native shores, to sojourn for years in lands where nothing but a popular adage—

" It is ill-omened to slay a Hindu, a Jew, a woman, and a dog"—

preserves him from destruction. And when he returns from the lands of the Mlenchha,* he is honoured instead of being excommunicated by his fellows. As he is accustomed to long voyages, instead of crunching parched grain, like the Indian, he sits down, on board ship, and " cooks bread." The diet prescribed by his religion being unsuited to the nature of the cold countries he adopts, it is quietly laid aside for one more generous and cosmopolitic. So also he has diminished his ablutions, extended his potations, and in many other little ways so dressed and trimmed his original rigid Hindooism, that it has become as presentable a thing as its natural awkwardness permits it to be.

The Banyan receives but a scanty education. After learning a few religious notions and cere-monies, quackeries and nostrums, he goes to a schoolmaster, who teaches him to read and write the alphabet, and explains the mysteries of the character which enters into his father's books, to add and multiply only—subtraction and division

* An Infidel, *i.e.* one not a Hindoo.

being considered *de trop*—and to indite a formal letter of business. Nothing can be ruder than the symbols which denote his complicated accounts: it is a system of stenography which admits none but initial vowels and confounds the appearance of nearly a dozen distinct consonants. These conclude his course of study: he then takes his place in the shop, where, if you please, we will leave him to cheat and haggle, to spoil and adulterate, and to become as speedily rich by the practice of as much commercial rascality as he can pass off upon the world.

The Amils or government officers—a class, created by the ignorance and inability of the Moslem rulers —are the most influential, and, conventionally speaking, the most respectable body of Hindoos in Scinde. They are distinguished from their fellow-religionists by their attire. The bigotry of the court forbade them to shave their beards, or to wear turbans: they lost the right of placing the tilak on the forehead, and they were compelled to trim the long moustaches with which the Hindoo loves to garnish his upper lip. In the present day, although sumptuary and costume regulations are utterly out of date, they still affect the peculiar Scindian cap, the shirt under the cotton coat, and the wide drawers gathered in at the ancle, as in wear amongst the

Moslems. They are a light-complexioned, regular-featured, fine-looking race, athletic compared with their brethren, from the liberal use of a meat diet; somewhat corpulent in consequence of their predilection for sweets and clarified butter, uncommonly proud of their personal appearance, and not a little fond of rich dress.

The literary attainments of an Amil are not extensive. In his boyhood he is sent to a Moslem akhund, or pedagogue, and learns to speak, read, and write the Persian language, or rather the kind of Lingua Franca which passes for Persian among the educated classes in India and Scinde. His pronunciation is, *mutatis mutandis*, that of an Englishman speaking French with a purely British accent. His style is equally curious, as he learns grammar by rote, without ever dreaming of the difference betwixt a noun and a verb. In selecting words, he jumbles together the learned and unlearned, obsolete and neological, slang and pure provincialisms: not unfrequently when run hard for terminology, he quietly introduces a Scinde vocable with or without the benefit of a foreign termination. The effect may be compared to a sporting friend's, " Moi drinkerai with vous," addressed to a French *homo unius linguæ*. His ignorance of the difficult arbitrary idiom of the beautiful sonorous Persian is complete and striking. He translates the phraseology of his uncouth mother tongue literally into the literary language, and thus his speech is always ridiculous, and not unfrequently offensive, by producing some unintended, but unmistakable, *double entendre*. Imagine the effect of rendering, How do you do? by *Comment faites-vous?*

After laying in a moderate stock of words and sentences, the amil proceeds to the perusal of certain works upon the subject of petitions, addresses, and epistolary correspondence, not inferior in manner and matter to our "Complete Letter Writers." He learns by heart the directions, the beginnings, and the endings, the "Sir-I-have-the-honours;" and the "I-have-the-honour-to-remain-Sirs;" and by much diligence masters the important distinctions between "Sir-of-high-degree," and "Sir-of-exalted-station."* He then peruses a poet, and a romancer or two, with the view of "getting up" common places, and "cramming" quotations, which may be produced as a proof of a liberal education. His preparatory studies conclude with a few simple arithmetical rules.

Our amil now, by the assistance of a kinsman, or

---

* Ali shan, the former, is applied to nobles, gentlemen, and equals generally; Ali jah, the latter, to respectable persons and inferiors.

a friend, obtains permission to squat upon the floor
of some daftar or government office, amongst the
crowd of scribes and clerks there assembled.   The
aspirant, thus upon the point of entering "life,"
devotes the energies of his mind to mastering the
complicated tricks and devices in which his craft
deals, and his juvenile efforts are carefully seconded
by the precept and example of his seniors.   He
learns to read out a paper to his employer, altering
sentences and paragraphs to suit the sense he deter-
mines it to convey; and when acting secretary by
order, to jot down, without hesitation, exactly as
much or as little of what is dictated to him as may
chance to suit his purpose.*   He acquires the arts
of writing a good feigned hand, and of copying
documents with deceptive skill; he becomes dexterous
at making a fresh paper look old and worn, as a
London Jew at manufacturing a Guido; and he
practises till perfect, with laborious industry, the
many ways of forging a seal.†   This prelude to his
career concludes with the acquirement of considerable

---

* A system which nothing can check but an actual perusal of all letters
or the plan adopted by Tippoo Sultan. The ruler of the Mysore could
neither read nor write : so to obviate danger of deception, after dictating
his orders to one secretary, he sent him into a closet, and put the paper
into the hands of a second. If word had not been set down for word, the
head of the writer at once paid the penalty.

† The seal in Scinde as in many parts of the Eastern World, is what
the signature is in the West.

knowledge about the best and safest way of receiving and administering a bribe. He is now a moonshee,* prepared to do his duty to his master by deceiving him whenever deception is profitable, and to the government, that employs both, by plundering it to the utmost extent which his means and opportunities permit him.

The Scindee is the scribe's mother tongue, but as he never peruses the works which it contains he is ignorant of all beyond a mere colloquial knowledge of it. His private studies are of a religious nature. If he inclines to the faith of Nanah Shah, he learns to read and write certain passages of the Granth, or Sikh scripture. He prepares for himself a Pothi (prayer-book), but too idle to learn the Gurumukhi character,† he copies from some friend's breviary the select passages,—such as hymns to the Creator, to the Great Incarnation, to the Saints, and to the River, astrological tables, books of fate, formulas for calculating lucky and unlucky days, magical charms, and medicinal prescriptions,—in the Nastalik, or common Persian character.

* In Persia, the title of munshi (or moonshee, secretary) is given only to men of learning : in India every fellow who can read a page of Hindostanee, or scrawl a wretched note, arrogates unto himself the name.

† The Gurumukhi is the modification of the Devanagari, or Sanscrit alphabet, used in the Holy Writ of the Panjab.

Contrary to the usual practice of Hindoos, the amils marry late in life, in consequence, I believe, of the expense attendant upon their nuptial ceremonies. Some few live and die bachelors. Most of them are grossly immoral, addicted to gambling, and to the abuse of spirituous liquors. From mixing much with the members of another faith, and possessing a little more knowledge than their neighbours, many of these men become Dahri, or materialists, owning the existence of a Deity, but dissociating the idea from all revelation, and associating it with the eternity past and future of matter in its different modifications. A few are Atheists in the literal sense of the word, but it is rare that they will trust their secret to a stranger. All these freethinkers are formidable things. Infidelity, by which I understand the rejection of any local system of revealed religion, is less common in the unenlightened East than it is in the civilised West : but the European seldom thinks proper, or takes the trouble, to make converts to his disbelief; the Oriental does, and aided by his superiority in learning over the herd, he frequently does it with great success. To judge from the progress of the Sufi, or mystic tenets, in Persia, and the Vedantic philosophy in India, a mixture of pantheism with pure deism, will, presently, be the faith of the learned and polite in both those countries.

There are not many castes of Shudra, or Servile Hindoos, in Scinde; and the few that exist have adopted the Brahmanical thread,* the sectarian mark, the diet, dress, and manners of the Banyans. The principal trades are the wahun, who lives by toasting different kinds of grain;† the khatti, or dyer; the hajjam, who combines the employment of cupping and shaving; and the sochi, who makes cloth slippers, but leaves leather slippers to the impure mochi. ‡

In Hyderabad, and the other large towns, are several families of the mongrel religionists, called Sikhs. The wild tracts of country in the east of Scinde contain some curious tribes of outcasts, and in several parts of the province a variety of mendicant orders, as numerous as the begging friars of Southern Europe, exercise their offensive profession. This, the fluctuating population, not actually belonging to the region, I have minutely

* Like the Nairs of Malabar, and other similar castes in India, who together with the functions and employment, have taken to themselves the rights of a higher family.

† Many kinds of grain, such as rice, wheat, Bengal gram, holcus, and other cereals are boiled, dried, and washed upon iron plates, to be eaten on journeys, and at different religious epochs.

‡ The " tanner," an outcast who dresses and works leather.

described in an ethnological work upon the subject of Scinde.

Although the Hindoo's religion has, like the Moslem's, been contaminated by contact with strangers,* still there is no lack of bigotry in the land. The polytheist will often, for a consideration, or with an object, represent himself as inclining to Christianity; but not even once, as yet, has he taken the irrevocable step—the beefsteak, or the going to church. If he has nothing to gain by apparent attachment to the creed of his masters, he opposes strenuously enough everything that militates against his conviction and peculiar prejudices. A friend of mine, vaccinator in Scinde, found serious difficulties to contend with when he attempted to spread the blessing amongst the Hindoos of Kurrachee. The pagans believe small-pox to be a manifestation of the atrocious deity, Devi herself: they therefore bury instead of burning the victims to the malady, and look upon all precautionary measures as direct acts of hostile aggression upon the deity. Yet, as usual, they abound in contradictions: when a child falls sick, the father runs for a doctor as well as a priest;

* The Moslem and the Sikh. The latter is a heretic Hindoo, and therefore a more dangerous antagonist than the former, who attacks polytheism with all the violence of a monotheist.

and when he dies, he laments him not the less because he has died of a goddess.

The Hindoo women in Scinde are superior to their lords in personal appearance. Many of them are very pretty, with correct features, magnificent hair, elegant figures—though not free from the prevalent defect of India, high shoulders—and clear olive skins, sometimes lighted up with the faintest possible pink colour. Their beauty is ephemeral; and all of them, if they have enough to eat, and are not worked too hard, quadruped like, become fleshy and corpulent. A simple diet, a life spent almost in the open air, and an unartificial toilet, consisting, *in toto*, of a white veil thrown over the head, a loose boddice to conceal the bosom, a long and wide petticoat, and sometimes a pair of slippers, preserve them from the hundred nervous and hysterical ailments of dyspeptic civilisation.

The Hindoo ladies are less educated, but also less fond of pleasure,—which here means, feasting, hard drinking, and flirtation—than those of the Moslems.* Their vanity, the ruling passion of the fair, finds a safety valve in an extensive display of grotesque ornaments, metal rings in the ear, the nostril, the cartilage

* Except at Shikarpur.

of the nose, on the wrists and fingers, ankles, and toes, necklaces, and large ivory circles covering all the fore-arm. Being under strict surveillance, and hourly liable to bodily chastisement, administered with no sparing hand, they are good, hard-working, and affectionate wives. Their love for their offspring, the great female virtue in the East, is an all-absorbing passion, beautiful, despite of its excess. To the Hindoo mother her child is everything. From the hour of his birth she never leaves him day or night. If poor, she works, walking about with him on her hip : if rich, she spends life with him on her lap. When he is in health she passes her time in kneading, and straightening his limbs. When he is sick, she fasts and watches, and endures every self-imposed penance she can devise. She never speaks to or of him without imploring the blessing of Heaven upon his head ; and this strong love loses nought when the child ceases to be a toy; it is the mainspring of her conduct towards him throughout life. No wonder that in the East an unaffectionate son is a rare phenomenon : and no wonder that this people when offensively inclined always begin by abusing one another's mothers.

Own to me, Mr. Bull, if you have candour

enough, that in this point at least civilisation gains nothing by contrast with barbarism. The parents are engrossed by other cares—the search for riches, or the pursuit of pleasure—during the infancy of their offspring. In the troublesome days of childhood the boy is consigned to a nursery, or let loose to pass his time with his fellows as he best can; then comes youth accompanied by an exile to school and college; then the profession; then the marriage; and the " young family "—a *coup de grace*.

In civilisation, too, there is little community of interests and opinions between parent and child :— the absence of it is the want of a great tie. Often the former has authority over the latter, and abuses it; or the latter, being independent of the former, presumes upon it. The one may be a Roman Catholic and a Conservative; the other, a Methodist and a Free-trader: both are equally ready to fight " on principle " about their "principles." The contrary in these lands. · Opinions are heir-looms; religious tenets cannot differ; politics are confined to politicians; " principles " there are none, and every household feels—and moreover acts upon the instinct—that its only safeguard against the multitude of enemies without is unanimity within doors. *Every* houschold—excepting, of course, the great, all whose members arc rivals, and hate each other with the vivacious family hatred of Honourables, or Hibernians.

CHAPTER XIII.

THE SCINDIAN MAN—HIS CHARACTER AND WHAT HE DRINKS.

THE Scindian—by which I understand the mass of the population—is probably the descendant of the ancient Hindoo race that possessed the country, with a slight admixture of Arab, Beloch, Brahm and Affghan* blood in his veins. To this circumstance, doubtless, he owes his more muscular frame and robust general appearance : the connexion with the superior sub-family has, however, possibly from local causes, failed to produce a strictly speaking improved development. His complexion varies from a deep chocolate colour—the sign of the lower orders—to the darkest olive of Southern Europe in the higher classes : his features are not unfrequently regular and well cut ; the forehead, unlike the feeble brow of India, is high and arched: the aspect of the head is good, and nothing can be finer than the eyes, the hair, and the beard.

* Some allusion will be made to these races in a subsequent chapter.

The social position of the Scindian in his own country has for years been exactly parallel with that of the Saxon in England during the age that immediately followed the Norman invasion. Hence it is, that contrary to what might be expected from his physical superiority, his *morale* has sunk even below the average of Western India. His is emphatically a conquered race. Inhabiting a valley with a hot damp climate—the most unfavourable to manliness; exposed to the incursions of the hardy natives of the arid mountains that look down upon it, he had the bodily strength perhaps, but he had not the strong will, and he had not the vigour of mind to resist invasion, to emancipate himself from thraldom. Now, the contempt to which he has subjected himself by his self-conviction of inferiority, and the absence of any object which might infuse energy into his actions, have formed and fixed him a very slave.

The principal occupations of the settled Scindians are agriculture and manual labour. They own the worst land in the province, the tracts lying near the tails of canals, where the inundation seldom extends,* and the grounds cut off from land and

* Because the feoffees, whose estates lie about the head, will not take the trouble or go to the expense of excavating the beds. The only remedy for this evil would be to confiscate the whole or part of the said estates.

water transit; whilst the Beloch feudal lords, and their throngs of vassals, have secured for themselves most of the fertile and productive spots. Generally speaking, they are miserably poor: theirs is a bald and squalid wretchedness which must be witnessed to be understood. I have seen whole families of the wretches picking up off the roads and highways the grains of barley they might chance to find there.

There are few districts in this part of Asia where the cultivators are not bankrupts, only prevented from failing, as it were, by its being the interest of the creditor not to ruin his debtor beyond a certain point. The way by which this comes to pass in Scinde is as follows:—The peasant paid one-third or one-half the produce of his fields to the ruler, ameer, governor, or commissioner: we will suppose that he paid it in kind, to make the hard condition as favourable as possible to him. Upon the other moiety or two-thirds, he and his family had not only to subsist the whole year round, but also out of it he was required to economise the wherewithal to sow his fields when the season came round. Here lay the difficulty. The peasant could not save; and if he could, he would not save:—so when seed was required, he went off to the Hindoo, the usurer and attorney of the little parish; and, after immense trouble, took up at the rate of about cent. per cent., mortgaging at the same time the coming harvest, the smallest quantity deemed necessary. He was then a ruined man.

Besides receiving an enormous rate of interest, the creditor who can read, write, and compute, turns the ignorance of his debtor to profit by keeping his accounts in a state of confusion most advantageous to the only one that understands them—himself. The wretched ryot *, after paying off his liabilities a dozen times or more, is still as deeply indebted as ever. Under the native rule it was, and under any system it would be, the same. As for discharging the debts of the community, and starting them, as the phrase is, " clear " in the world, I doubt whether the revenue of Great Britain would suffice to do it. Only where natives govern they keep up larger establishments—markets, as it were, for produce— than we do, and they will more easily remit the rate demandable from the agriculturist. The frequent wars, tumults, and invasions, too, have one good effect, the allowing ground to lie fallow for awhile.

The Hindoo's reed pen is a rod of iron, and

* In the Europeo-Asiatic jargon, the rayah is the Turkish—the ryot, the Indian, peasant: both, you would scarcely believe, the feat of Caco-graphy's, being one and the same Arabic word, رعيّة.

abjectly the unhappy Scindian trembles before it. I was forcibly struck by an example of its power on one occasion when travelling down Eastern Scinde. My tent was pitched near a little village; and the natives, who in those days considered every European a petty sovereign, were careful to come out *en masse*, and pay their respects to the hat and the shooting-jacket. Amongst the last visitors was a fair specimen of the race that hath been most unjustly designated as "mild and lowly;" a dirty, cringing Hindoo, with Shylock written in every line of his cold, lean, greedy countenance. Standing up humbly enough, he began to detail his grievances, insisting particularly upon the bad conduct of some unhappy Mussulman ryot, who would not pay his debts legally contracted.

"Hast thou seized his corn?" I asked.

"Of course, great Rajah: but it is not enough!"

"Hast thou sold his cattle?" (without them the poor wretch could not plough a square foot of field).

"Certainly. Long may your Rajahship flourish! but he still owes me rupees."

"Hast thou taken his wife's jewels, their clothes, the ornaments of their children, their furniture, &c.?"

"Yes; but he was so poor—what were the things worth?"

" And thou hast not turned him out of house and home, thou —— "

" He sits in the jungle, great prince."

" Then, man of dense brains, what wouldst thou have me do?—what wouldst thou do thyself?"

My friend was evidently of opinion that by science and vigour blood might be extracted from a turnip; and he hinted not obscurely at a mode of torture, which he assured me, under the native princes, was never known to fail. From his account of it I should agree with him, the alternative being literally pay or die. In vain I attempted to illustrate the homely proverb above quoted;—in vain I represented, that we civilised Europeans allow no corporeal punishment for debt—only a compulsory residence in certain government bungalows. My Hindoo affected to believe what I was saying: he left me, however, not daring to grumble, but looking his profound dissatisfaction at having come across so thick-headed, and at the same time so imaginative, a conqueror.

In the East, Mr. Bull, such a scene is impressive.

The nomadic Scindians who inhabit the hills in the western, and the oases in the deserts of the eastern frontier, are taller, stouter, and hardier men than those settled upon the plains of the Indus. In appearance many of them are scarcely to be distinguished from their Beloch neighbours; and the latter, in some cases, have learned to respect their strength and fitful valour. They live by fishing and hunting, by breeding horses, camels, and sheep, by resorting to the low country for employment, when agriculture is at a standstill, and by cultivating little patches of ground sufficient to provide them and their families with food.

The Scindian's daily bread is a thick, flabby cake of bajri* flour, flavoured with salt, mixed with water, well kneaded and baked without leaven on a clay plate, reeking with rancid butter, greenish in colour, and of particularly uninviting taste. It is considered very heating, so the people almost live upon it during the cold weather. For the rich there are about fifteen kinds of "rot †," as the stuff is most appropriately called, made of different grains, or cooked in particular ways; some of them, the sweet ones, rather resembling buttered toast, coated with coarse brown sugar. The national drinks are milk and water, not mixed. The luxurious enjoy pillaus, dressed in a pseudo-

---

* A kind of grain, intelligibly described in dictionaries, "Penicillaria vulgaris." † Bread, in Scindee.

Persian style, fresh and dried fish, game, vegetables, fruits, and other delicacies. All smoke the hookah —in these regions a peculiar looking affair, composed of a large, roundish vessel of clay, baked red, with a long, thin neck, into which is inserted the stem that supports the chillam, or bowl. The smoke, passing through the water, is inhaled by means of a reed pipe that projects from the side of the reservoir. There are several varieties of tobacco : the best, called Shikarpuri, would, if properly cured,* form a valuable article of commerce.

One of the great causes of the Scindian's degeneracy is the prevalence of drunkenness throughout the province. All ranks and creeds, sexes and ages, drink; the exceptions being a few religious men and dames of godly lives. Oriental like, they sit down to their cups with the firm intention of disqualifying themselves for arising from them. There is little grape wine in the country, the fruit being rare, and generally used for eating. The common alcohols are those distilled from molasses or dates, with the addition of a little mimosa bark, and other ingredients. When pure they are fiery as æther or sal volatile, and the novice hesitates which to abhor the

---

* It is terribly sweated by being stacked in cocks covered with matting so as to exclude the air : hence its inferiority of flavour.

most, the taste or the smell of the potion. Sometimes it is perfumed with musk, citron peel, rose flowers, or saffron, and the spirit is blunted by a plentiful admixture of molasses or sugar-candy.

The alcohols, however, like the wines and opium, are confined to the higher orders, and those who can afford such luxuries.* The common people must content themselves with the many preparations of the deleterious bhang, in England called Indian hemp †; and so habituated have they become to it, that, like drinkers of laudanum, they can scarcely exist without it. Near all the large towns there are particular places, called daira ‡, where regular drunkards assemble to debauch in public. The building is one large, open room, generally in a garden, planted with basil and other odoriferous plants; there must be a lofty wall to exclude the gaze of passers by; but spreading trees, and a bubbling stream—the scene in which the Persian

* The nobles infinitely prefer European preparations, especially the strong and sweet—as curaçoa and noyau. Some of the Parsees who traded in these articles when we first took the country, made considerable sums of money.

† Bhang (in Persian, bang), is the name of the herb, and also of the favourite preparation of it described below.

‡ Our government has wisely taxed the hemp which, under the native princes, almost every peasant grew for himself. The daira should be licensed or limited in numbers by some means or other, as they are most prejudicial to the well-being of the people.

loves to wrestle with Bacchus—are rare luxuries in this land. About sunset, when the work of the day is happily over, the bhangis* begin to congregate, each bringing with him his hemp, his pipkin, his " staff †," and the other necessaries. Then ensues a happy half-hour of anticipation. All employ themselves in washing out the leaves with "three waters," in pressing the mass between the palms—blessing it lustily the while—in rubbing it with the pestle in the brass pot-full of water or milk, and in sweetening the nauseous draught, with irrepressible glee at the nearing prospect of their favourite occupation. After drinking or smoking the drug, the revellers fasten on the hookahs placed upon the floor, and between the puffs either eat little squares of sweetmeat, to increase the intoxication, or chew parched grain to moderate its effects. In about half an hour the action of the drug commences : each man is affected by it in a somewhat different way. One squats, stupid and torpid, with his arms wound round his knees, and his long beard shaking, like a goat's when browsing, with every nod of his falling

---

* An habitual bhang-drinker is termed a bhangí, and the name is considered light and slighting even by those who indulge in the forbidden pleasure.

† Asá is the native word for the dwarf club with which they triturate and mix the small leaves, husks, and seeds of the plant with milk or water.

head. His neighbour may prefer a display of musical skill, in which he perseveres solely for his own benefit. Another, delighting in privacy, throws a sheet over his head, and sits in a corner of the room, meditating intensely upon the subject of nothing. A third talks disjointed nonsense; a fourth, becoming excited, will begin to perform a *pas seul,*—if of choleric complexion he will, Irishman like, do all he can to break some dear friend's head. And the multitude, the "old hands," sit quietly looking on, occasionally chatting, and now and then entertaining one another with lies the most improbable, incoherent, and grotesque, that ever shifted from mortal lips to mortal ears. There is one remarkable peculiarity in the assembly. If a single individual happen to cough or to laugh, the rest, no matter how many, are sure to follow his example. And the effects of the continuous and causeless convulsions of the lungs and cachinnatory muscles upon a bye-stander—not drunk—is exceedingly striking.

The social meeting usually breaks up about 8 P.M., at which hour the members with melancholy countenances retire to their suppers and their beds.

You have read, I suppose, Mr. Bull, some execrable translation of a certain spirit-stirring tale

—Monte Christo. Perhaps you remember that truly Gallican part of it in which the hero administers Hashish* to his friend, and the very romantic description of what the Hashish did to that friend. You must know that these are the effects of hemp and books, in the regions of imagination, in the world of authorism—a strange place where men are generous, women constant, the young wise, the old benevolent—not in the deserts of actuality. I have often taken the drug, rather for curiosity to discover what its attractions might be, than for aught of pleasurable I ever experienced. The taste of the potion is exactly what a mixture of milk, sugar, pounded black pepper, and a few spices would produce. The first result is a contraction of the nerves of the throat, which is anything but agreeable. Presently the brain becomes affected; you feel an extraordinary lightness of head as it were; your sight settles upon one object, obstinately refusing to abandon it; your other senses become unusually acute—uncomfortably sensible—and you feel a ting- . ling which shoots like an electric shock down your limbs till it voids itself through the extremities. You may stand in the burning sunshine without

* The Arabic name for Indian hemp when prepared.

being conscious of heat, and every sharp pain is instantly dulled. Your cautiousness and your reflective organs are painfully stimulated; you fear every thing and every body, even the man who shared the cup with you, and the servant who prepared it; you suspect treachery every where, and in the simplest action detect objects the most complexedly villainous. Your thoughts become wild and incoherent, your fancy runs frantic; if you are a poet, you will acknowledge an admirable frame of mind for writing such " nonsense verses," as the following :—

"The teeth of the mountains were set on edge by the eating of betel,
  Which caused the sea to grin at the beard of the sky." *

If you happen to exceed a little, the confusion of your ideas and the disorder of your imagination will become intense. I recollect on one occasion being persuaded that my leg was revolving upon its knee as an axis, and could distinctly feel as well as hear it strike against and pass through the shoulder during each revolution. Any one may make you suffer agony by simply remarking that a particular

* Dr. Herklots (Qanoon-e-Islam) quotes these lines as an " enigma," and gravely explains the signification which he supposes them to bear. They form part of a poem consisting of " nonsense verses "—a favourite mode of trifling in the East, and composed, men say, under the influence of bhang.

limb must be in great pain, and you catch at every hint thrown out to you, nurse it and cherish it with a fixed and morbid eagerness that savours strongly of insanity. This state is a very dangerous one, especially to a novice; madness and catalepsy being by no means uncommon terminations to it. The generally used restoratives are a wine glass full of pure lemon juice, half-a-dozen young cucumbers eaten raw, and a few puffs of the hookah; you may conceive the state of your unhappy stomach after the reception of these remedies. Even without them you generally suffer from severe indigestion, for during the intoxication of bhang, the unnatural hunger which it produces excites you to eat a supper sufficient for two days with ordinary circumstances.

These are the effects popularly associated by the Orientals with drinking bhang and those which I myself experienced. Almost every bhangi however feels something that differs from the sensations of his neighbour. And of course the more habituated a man becomes to the use of the drug, the more pleasurable he finds the excitement it produces. It has two consequences which appear to vary only in degree—fearfulness during' the fit, and indigestion after it.

In consequence of the extensive use made of the

preparation by the mystics of the East and the multitudinous visions and presences with which their maudlin moments have been enlivened, the drinking of " verdure," (Sabzeh) as the Persians call it, is considered by ignorant free-thinkers a kind of semi-religious exercise. A Sufi bard thus addresses his *poculum*, allegorising its spirit as well as its matter, its inner contents and outward form.

I.

O of heroic deed and thought sublime
And words of fire, mysterious fosterer,
        Imagination's font *
        And Inspiration's nurse !

II.

To the dull Past thou lend'st a rosier tinge,
Brighter bright Hope emergeth from thy stream,
        And dipped in thee, young Love
        Glows with a holier flame.

III.

Gaunt Poverty, grim Misery love to find
In thee their best, their sole mediciner.
        Thy potent spell alone
        Can smooth Pain's horrent brow.

IV.

And, Siren bowl, in thee the sage beholding
Types not obscure of matter's shifting scenes,
        Of deepest thought derives
        Sad salutary stores.

---

* In the original, " Sabgh,"—an allusion to Christian Baptism.

V.

Above eternity, without beginning,
Below thee lies eternity unending : •
    Thy narrow walls pourtray
    The puny bounds of Time.

VI.

Within whose circlet lies the world—a speck
Upon th' immense of being, like the mote
    That momentary beams
    In day's all-seeing eye.

VII.

And on thy brim the drops so passing sweet,
Withal so bitter in their consequence ;
    In them, friend, mind'st thou not
    Life's clogging pleasances ?

VIII.

Man is the heedless fly that comes and goes,
Flutt'ring his little hour of age away,
    Till, passing to his doom,
    Place knoweth him no more.

IX.

The annals of the world one tale repeat,
" At such a moment such a one expired."
    Of this all mindful live—
    Mirza,† prepared to die.

The almost universal use of Bhang throughout
the province has doubtless much to do with the

---

* The Moslems have cut "eternity" into two halves—Azaliyat
" beginninglessness," and Abadiyat " endlessness."

† The name of the bard who addresses himself, *more Persico,* at the
end of his ode. His poetry might be improved, as regards the working
out his metaphor. I leave it intact as a specimen.

Scindian's natural vices, inertness and cowardice, lying and gasconading. *Lente,* without the *festina,* has now become his motto for the management of life. The herdsman passes his day under a bush, alternately smoking, drinking hemp, dozing and playing upon the reed. The "navvy" on the canals—a large class in these regions—scratches up the mud with a diminutive hoe, deposits it in a dwarf basket, toils up the bank at the rate of a hundred yards an hour, and after concluding each laborious trip sits down groaning heavily to recreate himself with a pipe and to meditate upon approaching happiness in the form of "Bhang." Your boatman on the river will, if you permit him, moor his craft at noon regularly to enjoy his cups, and not to get through his work too quickly. So it is with the peasant at his plough, the huntsman, the fisher, the workman, the shopman, in a word with everybody.

The Moguls in ancient times used to curtail the lives of state prisoners by giving them every day before breakfast a cup full of what is called "Post." A dried poppy-head or two was infused in warm water allowed to stand the whole night, and in the morning squeezed till none of the juice remained in it. The draught was cooled with ice or snow in the hot weather—admire the exquisite delicacy of Indian politeness—sweetened, perfumed, and then administered to the captive. After a few months his frame became emaciated, his mind torpid and inert; and these symptoms did not cease developing themselves till death was the result of the slow poison. The Scindian by drinking his Bhang after dinner instead of before breakfast, allows himself some chance against the destroyer, but his health, bodily and mental, cannot but suffer from its certain effects.

The Scindians, like the unhappy Italians of modern days, have for generations felt the weight of foreign fetters; unlike the ancient Anglo-Saxons, they have none of the glorious phlegm and sturdiness with which the northern bore, without succumbing to, the *execrabile onus* of a master's arm. A race of slaves is not necessarily cowardly: witness the Nubian and other African bondsmen, than whom the world does not contain a more determined, dogged, and desperate set of ruffians. But the Scindian is constitutionally a poltroon:* his timidity is the double one of mind and body. An exception to the general rules of oriental resignation and Moslem fortitude,

---

* This remark by no means applies to the wild tribes of Scindians; and superior climate and the habit of danger have made many of them— the Jakhras, for instance—almost as brave as Belooches.

he cannot talk or think of death without betraying an abject grovelling fear, and even his Bhang will not give him courage to face the bayonet with common manliness.

Their preponderating development of cautiousness may account for the lying and vaunting propensities of the people. They deceive, because they fear to trust. They boast, because they have a hope of effecting by "sayings" what there are no "doings" to do. The habit soon becomes a confirmed one, especially amongst Easterns, who exaggerate and overdraw every thing in pure hate of nature and things natural. "Shahbash Pahlawan," go it my *heroes!* cries the Tindal or skipper of your Dhundhi,* at every stroke of the sweep handled by his trembling "braves." If a score of naked boors congregate in a dirty village, they will call it a "Shehr," a city. The chief of a petty tribe must prefix the title of "Malik," king, to his ignoble and cacophonous name. Your escort—half a dozen ragged matchlock men—dubs itself a "Lashkar," an army; and when you ride over to some great man's palace, accompanied by a single domestic, your groom is gravely termed your "Sawari," or retinue. The noble boasts that his clan musters 50,000 men, all

* A kind of craft upon the Indus. See chap. XXVIII.

perfect Rustams* or Camelfords for fighting : every individual of that 50,000 will, if you believe him, convince you that—

> " His joy is the foray, the fray his delight."

Take up a horsewhip, and the Rustam will infallibly decamp as fast as the portable armoury of weapons about his person allows him to do.   And so on with every rank and condition of man.

* The Persian hero : a kind of Hercules, Sampson, and Solomon combined : although a Pagan, he will escape eternal punishment by reason of his valour.

CHAPTER XIV.

THE SCINDIAN WOMAN—ESPECIALLY HER EXTERIOR.

In treating of the fair sex, we ought, I suppose'
Mr. Bull, to commence by a sketch of superficialities,
thereby suiting manner to matter.

The first thing the Eastern traveller home-
returned remarks in the streets of his native town
is, that scarcely any two people resemble each other.
In the most civilised European countries there has
been such a mixture of blood and breed that now an
almost infinite variety of features and complexions,
shapes and forms, has been grafted upon the original
stock which each region grew. He then explains
to himself how it was that during his earlier months
of wandering, he thought all the men he met
brothers, all the women sisters, and remembers
that, till his eye became familiar with its task, he
could trace no more distinction between individuals
than a cockney would discover in two white sheep
of a size.

Caste,* in this part of the Eastern world, groups the population of a country into so many distinct bodies, each bearing a peculiar likeness to the other, and all a general one to the characteristic face and form of the race. Rank makes some difference of colour—the higher it is the fairer the skin †—and wealth gives a delicacy of feature and figure—not to be found amongst the ill-fed, ill-clad, and hard-worked poor; but here they fail to destroy the family resemblance which naturally exists between individuals of the same country, age, and creed.

I must request you to be present at the unpacking of a Scindian lady of high degree, during which operation I shall lecture upon the points most likely to interest you, sir, my intelligent audience.

Observe, she stands before you in her Burka—ungraceful prototype of the most graceful mantilla—which has frequently, and not inaptly, been compared to a shroud. Its breadth at the shoulders, narrowing off towards the feet, makes it look uncommonly like a coffin covered with canvas: the romantically inclined detect a " solemn and nunlike appearance in

* This corrupted Portuguese word (*casta*) may venially be applied to the half Hindoo Mussulman of Scinde and India ; though, properly speaking, no such distinction prevails in the world of Islam.

† So much so that a Hadis or traditional saying of the prophet's declares that none of his descendants shall be a dark-coloured man.

the costume," and the superstitious opine that the figure thus arrayed "looks like a ghost." The material is thick cotton cloth, which ought to be white, but is like a Suliote's frock, " *d'une blancheur problématique ;* " a strip of coarse net, worked lattice-wise, with the small *œils de bœuf* opposite the eyes, covers and conceals the face. This article is a great test of "respectability," and is worn in token of much modesty and decorum. Satirical Scindians, however, are in the habit of declaring that it is a bit of rank prudery, and that the wearer of the Burka, so far from being better, is generally a little worse than her neighbours. Our lady is very strict, you may see, in "keeping up appearances;" for in addition to the mantilla, she wears out of doors a long wide cotton *Paro,* or petticoat, for fear that chance should expose the tips of her crimsoned toes to a strange man's gaze.

She is now in her indoor costume. Over her head, extending down to the waist behind, is a veil of Tattah silk, with a rich edging, the whole of red colour, to denote that the wearer is a " happy wife."* The next garment is a long wide shift, opening in front, somewhat after the fashion of a Frenchman's

* " Subhagan" is the native word: widows and old ladies generally dress in white.

blouse ; the hanging sleeves are enormous, and a richly-worked band or gorget confines it round the throat. At this season of the year it is made of expensive brocade, in summer Multan muslin would be the fashionable stuff. There are no stays to spoil the shape : their *locum tenens* is a harmless spencer or boddice * of velvet, fitting as tight as possible to the form, concealing the bosom, and fastening behind. The " terminations," of blue satin, are huge bags, very wide behind, to act as *polisson* or *crinoline*, and narrowing towards the extremities sufficiently to prevent their falling over the foot. These are gathered in at the ancles, and correct taste requires this part to be so tight that our lady never takes less than twenty minutes to invest her fair limbs in her *Sutthan*, or pantaloons. I must call upon you to admire the *Naro*, or trowser-string : it is a cord of silk and gold, plaited together with a circle of pearls at both ends, surrounding a ruby or some such stone, set in wire, concealed by the coils of the pendant extremities. Concludes the toilette with slippers, a leathern sole, destitute of hind-quarters, whose tiny vamp hardly covers the toes : its ornaments are large tufts of floss silk, various coloured foils, wings of green beetles, embroidered,

* In shape and duty resembles the Roman *Strophium.*

or seed pearls sewed upon a bright cloth ground. To see the wearer tripping and stumbling at every second step, you would imagine that the Scindian, like the subject of the Celestial Empire, had knowingly put a limit to his lady's power of locomotion. But no, sir, it is only "the fashion"—licensed ridiculousness.

A red silk veil, a frock of white muslin, through which peeps a boddice of crimson velvet and blue satin pantaloons : own that though the lady's costume is utterly at variance with *Le Follet,* and would drive *Le Petit Courier* into a state of demency, it is by no means wanting in a certain picturesque attractiveness.

And now for the lady's *personale.* Her long, fine jetty hair, perfumed with jessamine and other oils, is plastered over a well-arched forehead, in broad flat bands, by means of a mixture of gum and water. Behind, the *chevelure* is collected into one large tail, which frequently hangs down below the waist, and—chief of many charms—never belonged to any other person : it is plaited with lines of red silk, resembling the trowser-string, and when the head, as frequently happens here, is well shaped, no coiffure can be prettier than this. Her eyes are large and full of fire, black and white as an onyx stone, of almond shape, with long drooping lashes, undeniably beautiful. I do not know exactly whether to approve of that setting of Kajal* which encircles the gems; it heightens the colour and defines the form, but also it exaggerates the eyes into becoming *the* feature of the face—which is not advisable. However, I dare not condemn it. Upon the brow and cheek bones a little powdered talc is applied with a pledget of cotton, to imitate perspiration—a horrible idea, borrowed from Persian poetry,—and to communicate, as the natives say, " salt " to the skin. The cheeks are slightly tinged with lac rouge, a vegetable compound which I strongly recommend, by means of you, Mr. Bull, to the artificial complexion-makers of the west. The nose is straight, and the thin nostrils are delicately turned. You, perhaps, do not, I do, admire their burden—a gold flower, formed like a buttercup, and encrusted with pearls; † at any rate, the bit of black ribbon which connects it with the front hair is

* Lampblack collected by holding a knife over the flame of a lamp and applied with a glass, leaden, or wooden needle, called a *Mil*, to the edges of the eyelids. This is the *fuligo* of the Roman ladies ; how is it that the Parisians have not yet tried it ?

† There are several kinds of nose ornaments, the usual ones are a large metal ring fixed in either wing, or a smaller one depending from the centre cartilage of the nose. When removed, a clove or a bit of silver of similar shape is inserted into the hole to prevent its closing.

strictly according to the canons of contrast. The
mouth is well formed, but somewhat sensual in its
appearance; the teeth are like two rows of jessamine
buds—the dentist and the dentifrice being things
unknown—and moles imitated with a needle dipped
in antimony give a *tricolor* effect to the oral region.
The lips and gums are stained with a bark called
Musag, which communicates an unnatural yellowish
tinge to them; it is not, however, so offensive to the
eye as the Missi * of India. As large ears are very
much admired, that member is flattened out so as to
present as extensive an exterior as possible. And
as pale palms and soles are considered hideous,
those parts, the nails included, are stained blood red
with henna leaf.† Finally, hair on the arms being

* A powder of vitriol, steel filings, and other ingredients. It is rubbed
into the roots of the teeth as an antiseptic, and a preservation against the
effects of the quicklime, chewed with betel nut; the colour is between
rust and verdigris—the appearance unnatural and offensive.

† This leaf has two effects upon the skin; it is an astringent as well as
a dye. Unlike the noxious metallic compounds of Europe it improves the
hair; the smell is not disagreeable, nor is the trouble of applying it great.
Orientals suppose that it spoils by keeping, but they are in error. When
leaving India, I took several bottles of it carefully corked or waxed, round
the Cape, and a five months' voyage did not injure their contents in any way.

To prepare it the dried leaves must be forcibly triturated in warm
water or rice gruel, ten or twelve hours before use; it should then be
placed for a while in the sun, or exposed to gentle heat. The paste is
applied with a brush—it stains the skin—from the roots to the point of the
hair when well cleaned with soap or pearlash: five or six hours suffice to
produce a deep brick-dust hue, which a paste of indigo-leaves speedily
converts into a jetty black.

held an unequivocal mark of low breeding, it is carefully removed by means of a certain depilatory called Nureh.* Our lady, you see, wears no stockings, but callosities and other complaints which call for the chiropodist are not likely to offend our eyes.

The costume I repeat is picturesque. There is, however, I must confess, something grotesque in the decoration of the person—uncivilised and semi-barbarous people can never rest content with the handywork of nature: they must gild refined gold, tattoo or tan, paint or patch a beautiful skin, dye or chip pearly teeth, and frizzle or powder "hyacinthine locks,"—deadly sins against taste, these "adulteries of art!"

In point of ornaments, the Scindian lady's taste is execrable. Polite Europe now owns that a Sevigné adds nothing to the charms of a fine forehead and takes nothing from the uncomeliness of an ugly one: that gold pendula affixed to the ears are vanities, and that a simple black velvet band is at least as becoming as circles of massive metal or gaudy stones.

---

* Made of yellow arsenic (1 oz.) pounded and mixed with quicklime (4 oz.) till the compound assumes an uniform yellowish tinge. It is applied to the skin in a paste made with warm water, and must be washed off after a minute or two, as it burns as well as stains. This admirable invention is ascribed by western authors to the ingenious Solyman, who could not endure to see the state of H. M. Bilkis of Sheba's bare legs.

But unhappily for polite Europe, although the daughter condemns as out of date what her mother delighted to wear, her daughter in her turn will certainly revert to it because her mother did not, her grandmother did, wear it. In the east there is none of this feeling. The comparative scantiness of the toilette calls for a number of ornaments which, like other things oriental, are neither changed nor renewed; handed down as heir-looms in the family, they form a considerable portion of its wealth, and are constantly accumulating—the interest upon the capital they absorb being the intense gratification which the proprietors experience in displaying them.

The popular frontal jewel is a ponderous concern of gold set with crystals or precious stones of any value. It is generally divided into three parts, a centre one occupying the middle of the forehead flanked by smaller end pieces that rest upon the temples. There is a lighter form of the same article, but both of them are too expensive to come within the means of the poor. The whole ear—lobe, helix and little ear—is so covered with weighty ornaments in the shape of gold rings, studs, jewelled or enamelled stars, and bell-like pendants, that it and its append-ages require to be supported with little chains. Varieties of the necklace are as disagreeably abundant. One kind is formed by simple or double strings of little or large beads of gold, silver, or glass threaded on silk : it is worn tight round the neck. Another is a similar ornament of embossed metal : another a solid collar, looking more like an instrument of punishment than a personal decoration. The finger rings are generally plain broad or narrow circles of metal: the rich ornament them with precious stones, and the very fashionable wear upon the thumb a little looking-glass, in which they are perpetually viewing their charms. On the arms,* besides a number of wristlets, bracelets, and armlets of gold, silver, or ivory, in the shape of rings, studs, flowers and chains, solid, hollow, or filled up with melted rosin, the lady generally carries about a talisman or two, † called a Tawiz, carefully preserved and justly considered the most valuable part of her trinkets. It is usually a slip of paper with a quotation from Holy Writ, some curious spell to avert the evileye, or a song to some dead saint, enclosed in a little silver case and fastened on by black silk threads, very old, brown and dirty. A friend of

* They never wear the Indian ornaments called "bangles"—thin rings of stained glass or sealing-wax—of which every well-dressed woman wears a dozen on each wrist.

† These are the "characts" of ancient days, commonly used in different parts of Europe.

mine who had earned local celebrity for writing them, showed me an ancient gentlewoman who for two years had borne the mystic words

"C——d Me,"

—of course in our vernacular—curiously and confusedly dispersed letter by letter throughout the squares, circles, and lozenges, in which the precious document abounded. And although my friend had on one occasion explained to the old lady in excellent Scindee, the purport of her "preservation," she insisting, wrong-headedly, as seniors at times will, upon the fact that she had worn the article in question during a very prosperous period of her life, decidedly refused to discard it.

The anklets as you see resemble the armlets in all points, except that they contain a greater mass of metal. Perhaps the prettiest is a silver ring set with a fringe of small circular bells which tinkle at every motion of the fair owner's foot. The rings on the toes have not an unpleasant effect, and the common ones of silver enamelled suit the colour of the henna remarkably well.

Now the Scindian lady stands before you in her veil, frock,—"chemisette" would sound prettier, but be decidedly incorrect,—boddice, pantaloons, and slippers; painted, patched, and dyed; be-ringed, be-neck-

laced and be-charmed literally from top to toe, both
parts included. Her attitude is not an ungraceful
one: she carries herself well, never stoops, and observe,
has not round shoulders. In her hand she holds a
silken string attached to a tassel that contains a bit
of musk, and to the nice conduct of this thing she
devotes much of her attention. In reply to our
salutations she raises the right hand—never the left
—to her forehead and briefly ejaculates "Salam."
If we ask her to sit down she will take a chair, but
being in the habit of squatting, she will certainly
place at least one foot upon the seat so as to imitate
as nearly as possible the position most natural to
her. If she drops her pocket-handkerchief, an
article of toilette used to be looked at not to use,
she is more likely to pick it up with her toes than
with her fingers—Easterns being all more or less
four-handed animals. In her continual adjust-
ment of her veil, I see a little ennui as well as
coquetting; she is tired of conversation, is not prepared for aught savouring of facetiousness, being
" upon her dignity," and longs for a pipe. Now,
whilst she is puffing it with immense satisfaction,
inhaling every atom with her lungs, and sedulously
displaying at the same time that she pretends to
conceal her arm and waist, I will oblige you with a

hasty biographical sketch as true to nature as I can make it.

Our visitor spent her early years in the harem, where she was frequently chastised by her mama, and where she scolded and romped with, pinched and scratched the slave girls, and conducted herself generally in a way which would have horrified the correct Mistress Chapone. At the early age of six she was mistress of the art of abuse and the rudiments of play*—here synonymous with cheating. Then commenced her education, she was taught to cut out and sew dresses, to knit and embroider, to repeat a few prayers, and as no expense was spared to make her perfect, a female pedagogue attended to teach her the reading of her mother tongue, and the letters rather than the words of the Koran. Of course she was not allowed to write, on account of the dangerous practices to which that attainment leads. But she wasted almost as much time as our young ladies do upon music; the only difference being that instead of eliciting dismal sounds from the pianoforte, she drummed upon the timbrel, and sedulously exercised her voice. From that somnific thing the drawing-master and the torments of the

---

* The games generally preferred are dice, cards, and several kinds of backgammon played with cowries.

professor of dancing she was spared; the former being
yet to be, the latter a purely professional, and by no
means a respectable person in this part of the world.

Her tenth year found her prepared, in mind, to
become a matron, and eagerly enough she looked
forward to the change, because she suspected that
in the holy state her liberty would not be so sadly
curtailed. One of her father's neighbours determined to obtain her for his boy; not because either
father or son had seen, admired, or loved the child,
but the connection appeared a good one, and the
youngster was old enough for a wife. So a lady
Mercury was despatched to the mother of the future
bride with many compliments, and most stringent
orders to remark the furniture of the house, the
conduct of its inmates, and particularly the age,
countenance, complexion, demeanour, gait, manners,
and accomplishments of the daughter. The latter
on the other hand was warned by her parent to
conduct herself with the nicest decorum, to squat
with her veil almost covering her head, never to
reply till addressed two or three times, and by
no means to spit; as her vivacity appeared likely
to get the better of prudence, she was soundly
slapped to induce a grave and reflective turn of
mind.

The visit passed off well, without, however, any thing being concluded. The Wakil* hinted at the object of the call, but her hosts being people of distinction, merely replied with the falsehood of *convenance*, that they " had no present intention of marrying their daughter." This, the artistic ambassadress, who has grown old in the art of making every one's business her own, knew perfectly well,— meant that they intended doing so at the first possible opportunity. So she returned to her employer and reported success.

As a second visit of the kind must not take place before a month has elapsed, the parents of the future couple spent their time in collecting all kinds of information about the young people from friends and neighbours, who systematically withheld it, because they expected a feast when the affair came off. The next *ambassade* was a decisive one, and a lucky day at a decent distance of time was fixed upon for the preliminary rite of betrothal.

On the evening appointed the boy's relations of both sexes assembled, and repaired with music and fireworks to the young lady's house, carrying a

* The Wakil, "go-between," or " Mrs. Gad-about," as this class is called by an English lady, who wrote an amusing and, curious to say, an accurate book about India. " Mrs. Mir Hassan Ali's Observations on the Mussulmans of India, 1832."

present of bijouterie and dresses. They found every thing prepared for their reception; the men's rooms were strewed with pipes, the Zenanah or Gynæceum was spread with the best carpets and hung with huge nosegays of strong scented flowers. The intended was publicly dressed in new clothes of the most expensive description, and ornamented with garlands, and the jewels sent by the bridegroom; henna was then placed upon her hands, and she was seated in a conspicuous part of the room, the centre of all attraction. There she continued for a while modestly confused with eyes fixed on the ground. Her mother then summoning the barber's wife, or rather the female barber—an important personage on these occasions—desired her to carry a pot of milk and a tray of sweetmeats into the gentlemen's apartments. This the old lady did, and with much jesting and railing made the party eat, drink, and be merry. She stayed with them till they all recited the Fatihah, or opening chapter of the Koran, with raised hands. The father of the bride who was concealing his intense delight at getting rid of the " household calamity," namely, a daughter, with a mingled expression of grief and shame, then appointed a day for the nuptial ceremony. Next took place a great fête, beginning with a feast, and ending with music and dancing; festivities continued for about a week, and with them concluded the preliminary of betrothal.

At this stage of the proceeding it is considered somewhat dishonourable to break off a match. At the same time there is no such nonsense in Islam as a suit for breach of promise—a demand for coins wherewith to salve broken heart and wounded feelings. Nor is there any religious impediment to a dissolution of the engagement. After the ceremony, as before it, the bridegroom is never, strictly speaking, allowed to see his intended; but as, all the world over, that formidable person, the mother-in-law, is at this stage of the proceedings disposed to regard her new son with favour, such events are by no means so rare as they should be.

The lady was married about a year after her betrothal, a delay politely long, as hurry towards matrimony is considered a suspicious sign. No sum of money that the family could afford was spared: feastings and merry-makings began a month or six weeks before the ceremony. All that Scindian art could do was put into requisition to make the bride look as pretty as possible. Cosmetics, oils, unguents, dyes, perfumes, depilatories, the paint brush, and the tweezers, were pressed into the service; each lady of the thousand visitors and every attendant abigail, having some infallible recipe for

" Enhancing charms—concealing ugliness,"

and with truly feminine pertinacity insisting upon trying it. The wonder was that, what with their vellications and shampooings, eternal bathings, and stuffings with churo,* rubbings with sandal wood and pitiless scourings with pithi,† they left the poor girl any beauty at all. Most of the torment was exhausted upon the lady: the hajjam or barber contented himself with " cleaning " the male patient, and the friends of the family exercised their active minds in dressing him up, so as to give him as much as possible the appearance of being a " gentlemanly-looking young man."

To describe all the now utterly meaningless puerilities and the succession of feasts that constituted the marriage in high life would be a task as tedious as it is profitless. Briefly to allude to them, both families kept open houses and invited all their relations morning and evening, eating, drinking, smoking and chatting all the day, and filling up the night with

* Churo, an unleavened cake of wheaten flour made into dough with clarified butter, and mixed with brown sugar—a bilious mess, popularly supposed to increase the delicacy of the skin.

† A succedaneum for soap, composed of sweet oil and the flour of mash —a kind of phaseolus.

dances, in which professional performers displayed their charms, whilst bands of most unmusical instruments screamed, jingled and rattled outside the doors for the edification of the excluded vulgar. A number of presents passed between the bride and the bridegroom, a series of visits kept their relations, to use a native phrase, in the state of "washerman's dogs 'twixt house and pond."* Dresses and jewels were canvassed, prepared, tried on, and scrutinised with religious care; the bridal paraphernalia † consisting of clothes, garlands, dressing-cases, trinkets, and a number of articles of furniture, were sent by the gentleman to the lady, and finally expiatory ceremonies were performed so as to defeat all the malevolent intentions of the fiend and the evil-eye.

Next came the Church's part of the solemnity. On the evening appointed, the cazee, or the mulla, was requested to be present at the house of the bridegroom's father, where there was a gathering of both families, the female sex, however, being strictly excluded. Then the priest, in set phrase, thrice

* Literally, " belonging neither to house nor ghaut"—a laundry-place, upon the steps of which the men of suds are wont to ply their vocation.

† This is the jahez, or dowry. It is the lady's property, descends to her children, and in case of her dying without issue belongs to her nearest of kin. The settlement made by the bridegroom is called the mahr. It is a religious obligation, without which no marriage is lawful : as, however, the bride is allowed to remit an indefinite portion of it, it is more generally owed than paid.

asked the young lady's parent, who had constituted himself her trustee, whether he agreed to marry his daughter to such and such a person. He responded solemnly in the affirmative. Upon this the marriage settlements were made; and as the father of the bride wished to give as little and to receive as much as possible; moreover as, strange to relate, the father of the bridegroom seemed possessed by a spirit of direct opposition to his future connection, the scene that ensued was an animated, but by no means a decorous one. It ended in the old way, when a thing must be done, by both parties giving up a little to each other. Then the cazee, rising from his seat, began to recite Arabic prayers, benedictions, the nuptial contract, and certain chapters of the Koran, setting forth the beauties of matrimony, and the lovely lives of hen-pecked patriarchs and prophets. Concluded this affecting part of the rite with a general congratulation and a heavy pull upon the father of the bridegroom's purse by the holy man,* and all those who could find the least pretext to assist them in the operation. Presents of camels, horses, gold-hilted swords, dresses of honour, ornaments, and

---

* The Koran does not permit cazees to take fees for marrying, reading prayers to, and burying the Faithful. Revelation having been unaccommodating in this little matter, the holy men are obliged to content themselves with daily pay, occasional presents, and grants of land.

jewellery, were showered about in such profusion that even to the present day the poor man feels the effects of a liberality, which nothing could have provoked but the absolute certainty, that upon it depended for existence his own good name and the respect of all his fellows.

Presently the nocturnal procession took place. The bridegroom was bathed, dressed, garlanded, and adorned with all the attention due to so important an occasion. Mounted on a white horse, and surrounded by a crowd of relations, friends, and spectators, with flags and fireworks, musicians, gymnasts, and dancing girls, he paraded through the streets, visited the mosque if he had time, and at last reached the bride's house. He then dismounted and was led or carried into the court-yard, where the women of the family received him: he entered the male assembly, and was almost immediately removed to the zenanah, where the lady awaited his coming. A number of uninteresting cere-monies followed, and, finally, the "happy couple" were left together with the pleasant certainty that at dawn they must surely rise to bathe, dress, say their prayers, and receive the congratulations of their friends.

Our Scindian lady—she signifies that she wants

another pipe—then entered upon life in real **earnest.**
She was permitted by her religion to call upon her
parents once a week;* she did so once a day, sometimes twice, and her husband, as might be **expected,**
felt the results.   Availing herself of the privilege of
womanhood, she added smoking and the **chewing of**
betel-nut to her other accomplishments.   She **spent**
her hours in decorating herself, not to fascinate the
eye of her spouse as she ought to have done, **but**
with the strictly feminine object of exciting the **envy,**
hate, and malice of all her dear family, friends **and**
acquaintances, by a display of dresses.   She punctu-
ally attended all feastings and junketings, nor **did**
she neglect the fairs at the tombs of saints, **and**
other religious assemblies, where religion is **usually**
the thing least thought of.   She had promised, **not**
as our ladies do, but by proxy, to " love, honour, **and**
obey," her goodman: she did neither this, that, **nor**
the other.   Old Saadi, the Oriental moralist—**about**
as moral a writer, by-the-by, as Pietro Aretino, **or**
Pigault Lebrun—makes it the test of respectability
in a house, that woman's voice should never be **heard**
beyond its walls.   The fair Scindian knows **nought**

* Before the birth of the first child.   All the terrors of religion, **stripes**
included, are directed against the wife who dares to visit her **parents**
without her husband's order.   What can the poor woman do but **duly**
and openly disobey them ?

of Saadi, and cares about as much for his tests and his opinions: she scolded her husband with womanly vigour, loudly and unrespectably at all hours.

After the birth of the first child the *petites misères de la vie conjugale* began to gather. The lady had been indulging a little too freely in the pleasures of— brandy. Her spouse discovered the circumstance, and chastised her corporally for the same. He should have begun that discipline earlier. Instead of bowing her head, she remarked that his face was a " black creation of God's." He, highly indignant at the truth of the observation, retorted by many a curse in query-form, to which she replied cate- gorically. A furious quarrel was the result. Fortu- nately for our visitor, Scinde then belonged to a civilised people, who systematically hang every man that kills his better half.* When the couple retired to rest that night, the husband, reflecting for the first time upon the blessings of polygamy, half determined to take to himself a second wife, and the lady indignantly running over the list of her grievances, firmly resolved to provide herself with a

---

* The Koranic law concerning adultery is utterly inadequate for the moral wants of any community—hence the use of the sack or the scimitar in Islam. Where we rule we should remember that taking away a man's only means to secure his honour, it is our duty to provide him with some other preservation, which generally speaking, we have not done.

cicisbeo. She would have demanded divorce from " that man " but for two reasons; in the first place, by such step, she would have forfeited all her claims to the mahr, or settlement; and secondly, she did not anticipate much happiness in returning home to be scolded by her mother, lectured by her father, snubbed by her brothers, and be sedulously watched and guarded by all. But she did not fail, knowing how much it would annoy her husband, to call upon " dear ma " as often as possible, to detail all her miseries, and to throw " dear ma's " words in his face at every opportunity. Finally, she threatened him with her father, and complained to her brothers with such assiduity, that the spouse, quite *excédé,* presently provided her with a lawful rival, she him with an unlawful one.

In Moslem countries polygamy is the exception, not the rule. It is confined to the upper and middle classes, who can afford themselves the luxury, and a first wife is seldom superseded unless issue be wanting, or incompatibility of temper render the measure advisable. The equitable law of the Koran concerning the marriage-settlement effectually prevents the abuse of divorce on an extensive scale; for a few rich nobles may, the many poor cannot, afford to pay the fortune of every woman they wish to put out of the house. Wives are limited to four—the number fixed by the Koran, and approved of by experience. One wife quarrels with you; two are sure to involve you in their squabbles, which end only to recommence, because they are equally matched; and when you have three a faction is always formed against her you love best, so as to make her hours bitter. But four find society and occupation for themselves; of course they divide into two parties, but you, oh husband, are comparatively comfortable.

How very selfish men are !

You must not run away with the opinion, Mr. John Bull, that these four ladies all occupy the same apartments. Were that the case, there would soon be murder in the house. Each has her own suite of rooms, her attendants, and her private establishment. In their intercourse there is much ceremony; no lady calls upon her neighbour without sending a previous message, and the relatives, friends, and acquaintances of the one are not expected to show any attention to the other. A certain amount of discipline is maintained by the first wife, who generally commands the female brigade, and the law of the Koran condemns the Moslem that allows himself to feel an undue partiality for any one of his four spouses. Fortunately

for Scinde, the fair sex is not skilful in toxicology
as are the dark dames of India, nor have they the
stout hearts and sturdy arms which often render the
burly beauties of Affghanistan truly formidable to
their husbands.

After what I have told you about our visitor, you
will readily believe that she is not so good a
mother as the Hindoo woman is. She considers every
child a disadvantage, as it robs her of the freshness
of her charms. She has to make the most of her
time, expecting to be an old woman at thirty, and
maternal duties are apt sadly to interfere with the
pursuit of excitement, and the enjoyment of pleasure.
But she also feels that her position in society—and
what will not a woman do for position?—mainly
depends for existence and continuance upon her offspring. If she has not a son, as soon as wrinkles
appear she will be cast aside like an antiquated piece
of furniture, doomed to the lumber-room till it falls
to dust. Her rival, against whom she has fought
through life—all for hate of course, not for love, with
the spirit of a heroine, and the zeal of a Jesuit—will
gloriously win the day: her husband will despise her
till he forgets her; her family will neglect her as a
most unprofitable person; briefly, there is no knowing
how dark her future fate may be. So she does not

utterly neglect her children; in their infancy she sees
that they are fed and bathed, and, as they grow
older, she takes more care of them; they become
the weapons with which she hopes, by Allah's aid, to
drive the fellow wife out of the well-fought field.

Soon our Scindian lady, after prolonging the evil
day as much as possible, will turn her back upon
pleasure, and apply herself either to unremitting
intrigue for the benefit of her offspring, or become
very devout and very disagreeable, inveighing bitterly
against the vanities of the world—for the usual reason,
because she can no longer enjoy them; and censuring
the "young people of the present day" because she
belongs to another generation. Her son and her
daughter will grow up; she will become a mother-
in-law in her turn. Then her husband will pass
away; she removes her ornaments, refrains from
perfumes and scented oils, dresses herself in dirty
white garments, and traditionises about, and antici-
pates reunion with her poor dear Jan Mohammed,
exactly as if she had been a British matron. And so
on:—the lights wane—the stage darkens—the curtain
descends.

 END OF VOL. I.

LONDON:
BRADBURY AND EVANS, PRINTERS, WHITEFRIARS.

THE

STANDARD NOVELS AND ROMANCES.

Price Three Shillings and Sixpence each.

<table>
<tr><td>1. The Pilot—Cooper.</td><td>26. Simple Story, and Nature and Art
—Mrs. Inchbald.</td></tr>
</table>

STANDARD NOVELS AND ROMANCES.

RICHARD BENTLEY, NEW BURLINGTON STREET.

SD - #0018 - 140723 - C0 - 229/152/17 - PB - 9780282102975 - Gloss Lamination